STUDY GUIDE

Imprisoned

Faith in All Circumstances

Derek W.H. Thomas

LIGONIER MINISTRIES
Renew your Mind.
LIGONIER.ORG | 800-435-4343

421 Ligonier Court, Sanford, FL 32771
Email: info@ligonier.org

Printed in China.

Contents

Introduction

From Genesis to Revelation, there is no shortage of God's people who have found themselves imprisoned. For each one of these people, there are lessons to be learned that can be applied to any trying circumstance. In this teaching series, Dr. Derek W.H. Thomas journeys through Scripture to draw out these lessons to strengthen our faith in whatever circumstances we might find ourselves.

This study guide is a companion to the video teaching series. Whether you are using the DVDs, streaming the videos on Ligonier.org, or going through the course in Ligonier Connect, this resource is designed to help you make the most of the learning experience. For each message in the series, there is a corresponding lesson in this guide. Here is what you will find in each lesson:

INTRODUCTION	The introduction is a brief paragraph that summarizes the content covered in the lecture and considered in the study guide lesson. **How to use:** Use the introduction to each lesson to get a sense of the big picture before watching the video. Refer to these statements as you work through the study guide to remind yourself of what you have already covered and where you are headed.
LEARNING GOALS	The learning goals are the knowledge and skills that the study guide lesson will endeavor to equip you with as you work through the lecture content. **How to use:** Familiarize yourself with the goals of each lesson before engaging its contents. Keeping the overall purpose in mind as you watch each video and reflect on or discuss the questions will help you get the most out of each lesson.
KEY IDEAS	The key ideas are the major points or takeaways from the lecture. **How to use:** Use these ideas to prepare yourself for each lesson and to review previous lessons. They describe specifically the knowledge that each lecture is communicating.

REFLECTION & DISCUSSION QUESTIONS	The questions are the guided reflection and/or discussion component of the lesson that is intended to help you prepare for, process, and organize what you are learning. **How to use:** Reflect on individually or discuss in a group the questions in the order in which they appear in the lesson. The time stamps in the right margin indicate where the answers to questions during the video can be found.
PRAYER	The prayer section offers suggestions for how to close the lesson in prayer with respect to what was taught in the lecture. **How to use:** Consider using each lesson's prayer section as a guide to personal or group prayer. These sections follow the ACTS prayer model, which you can learn more about in R.C. Sproul's Crucial Questions booklet *Does Prayer Change Things?* This helpful guide is available as a free e-book at Ligonier.org.
REVIEW QUIZ	The review quiz is a set of six multiple-choice questions that appears at the end of each lesson. **How to use:** Use each quiz to check your comprehension and memory of the major points covered in each lecture. It will be most beneficial to your learning if you take a lesson's quiz either sometime between lessons or just before you begin the next lesson in the study guide.
ANSWER KEY	The answer key provides explanations for the reflection and discussion questions and answers to the multiple-choice questions in the review quiz. **How to use:** Use the answer key to check your own answers or when you do not know the answer. Note: Do not give in too quickly; struggling for a few moments to recall an answer reinforces it in your mind.

Study Schedules

The following table suggests four plans for working through the *Imprisoned* video teaching series and this companion study guide. Whether you are going through this series on your own or with a group, these schedules should help you plan your study path.

	Extended 14-Week Plan	Standard 12-Week Plan	Abbreviated 6-Week Plan	Intensive 4-Week Plan
Week	**Lesson**			
1	*	1	1 & 2	1–3
2	1	2	3 & 4	4–6
3	2	3	5 & 6	7–9
4	3	4	7 & 8	10–12
5	4	5	9 & 10	
6	5	6	11 & 12	
7	6	7		
8	7	8		
9	8	9		
10	9	10		
11	10	11		
12	11	12		
13	12			
14	*			

* For these weeks, rather than completing lessons, spend your time discussing and praying about your learning goals for the study (the first week) and the most valuable takeaways from the study (the last week).

1

God's Presence with Joseph

INTRODUCTION

The story of Joseph is a familiar one to many people, believers and unbelievers alike. Joseph is known for his dream, his coat of many colors, his slavery, and his forgiveness toward his brothers. Have you deeply considered the providence of God in Joseph's life and how this story fits into the bigger picture of God's plan of redemption? In this lesson, Dr. Thomas recounts God's presence with Joseph so that we might grow in our understanding of God's presence with us and His purposes in our own lives.

LEARNING GOALS

When you have finished this lesson, you should be able to:

- Identify God's presence with Joseph and His providential purposes
- Describe the temptation that Joseph faced and how he fought temptation

KEY IDEAS

- While God's purposes may not be clear in the moment, they are often seen when we look back and trace His hand throughout our circumstances.
- Scripture is full of the "Immanuel principle"—the idea that God is with us.
- God is faithful to transform, preserve, and use His people.

REFLECTION & DISCUSSION QUESTIONS

Before the Video

What Do You Think?

Take a moment to answer the following questions. They will prepare you for the lecture.

- Spend a moment thinking of the characters and stories in the Bible involving imprisonment. List the biblical characters who come to mind.

- What kinds of lessons do you think these biblical characters learned, and what lessons do you think we can learn from their stories today?

Scripture Reading

And we know that for those who love God all things work together for good, for those who are called according to his purpose. For those whom he foreknew he also predestined to be conformed to the image of his Son, in order that he might be the firstborn among many brothers.

—Romans 8:28–29

- What is God's purpose for the believer in all things?

During the Video

Answer the following questions while you watch the video. They will guide you through the lecture.

Joseph's Backstory *0:00–10:43*

- What phrase is repeated throughout Genesis 39 regarding God's presence in the midst of Joseph's trial?

- What was Joseph like as a young boy?

- Why was Joseph imprisoned?

Joseph's Imprisonment and God's Purposes *10:43–23:48*

- What three things does Dr. Thomas note about the temptation that Joseph faced?

- After Joseph reasons through the temptation, how does he act decisively?

- According to Dr. Thomas, in what three ways was God with Joseph and working throughout his story?

After the Video

Answer the following questions after you have finished the lecture. They will help you identify and summarize the major points.

- Consider what Joseph was like as a young boy and the transformation God wrought in him. How does God's work in Joseph throughout his life give hope to the believer today?

  If you are in a group, have the members reflect on how God has transformed and providentially preserved them. Ask them to give testimony to God's work and rejoice together, giving Him the glory for His faithfulness.

- For what purpose was God providentially preserving Joseph?

  If you are in a group, have the members discuss how they can look back at the mystery of providence and see God's purposes.

- Dr. Thomas shares the following quote by John Owen: "Set faith at work on Christ for the killing of your sins and you will, in God's good providence, live to see your lust dead at your feet." How does the Christian practice this?

  If you are in a group, ask the members to spend some time praying for one another. Have them pray that as individuals and as a group, they would "set faith at work on Christ." Pray that God would grant them faith, repentance, and perseverance.

PRAYER

Commit what you have learned from God's Word in this lesson to prayer.

- Praise God for being Immanuel, God with us.
- Confess the ways in which you have failed to acknowledge and trust God's presence and purposes in your life.
- Thank God for the biblical example that we have in Joseph and how this bolsters our faith.
- Ask God to preserve you for His purposes and to empower you in the fight against sin.

REVIEW QUIZ

Use these multiple-choice questions to measure what you learned from this lesson.

1. What was Joseph's dream when he was a young boy?
   a. That his family would bow down to him
   b. That he would become the ruler of Egypt
   c. That his family would live long in prosperity
   d. That he would receive a coat of many colors
2. Who does Dr. Thomas compare with Joseph because this man, too, faced imprisonment?
   a. John Owen
   b. John Bunyan
   c. Ralph Erskine
   d. William Cowper
3. What is *not* part of Joseph's reasoning in response to temptation?
   a. He reasons that it would be a sin against God.
   b. He reasons that it would be an abuse of trust bestowed on him.
   c. He reasons that it would be an offense against Potiphar as a husband.
   d. He reasons that it would mar his reputation and the favor he had been granted.
4. What did Joseph discover while he was in prison?
   a. His gift of interpreting dreams
   b. How to get released from prison
   c. How to rise to profound influence
   d. The reason that Potiphar's wife accused him
5. John Flavel wrote *The Mystery of Providence*. How does he say that providence is best "read" or understood?
   a. By praying
   b. By predicting what God will do
   c. By reading providence backwards
   d. By discerning God's purposes step by step
6. Trial is a sign of the absence or removal of God's presence.
   a. True
   b. False

Answer Key—God's Presence with Joseph

REFLECTION & DISCUSSION QUESTIONS

Before the Video

What Do You Think?

These are personal questions. The answers should be based on your own knowledge and experience.

Scripture Reading

- What is God's purpose for the believer in all things?

  Romans 8:28 is a well-known verse that many people can quote. Unfortunately, for some, it has lost its power and comfort because it's become so familiar and is not always connected to the following verse. According to verse 28, God's purpose for believers is good. The thought continues into verse 29, where Paul identifies believers' greatest good—that God will conform them to Christ's image. We see this in the life of Joseph. God uses the circumstances and trials to transform Joseph into a wise, godly man who can be used for God's purposes and glory—all the while for Joseph's good. So it is in our own lives.

During the Video

Joseph's Backstory

- What phrase is repeated throughout Genesis 39 regarding God's presence in the midst of Joseph's trial?

  Genesis 39:21 says, "But the LORD was with Joseph and showed him steadfast love and gave him favor in the sight of the keeper of the prison." The idea that God was with Joseph is repeated in verses 2, 3, 21, and 23. O. Palmer Robertson calls this the "Immanuel principle" whereby we understand that God is with us.

- What was Joseph like as a young boy?

  Joseph grew up in what we would call a "dysfunctional family." He was shown favoritism as a young boy. During his youth, Joseph was not exactly what we would consider a model Christian. Dr. Thomas points out how Joseph seems somewhat selfish, arrogant, and lacking in wisdom according to the accounts provided in Genesis.

- Why was Joseph imprisoned?

  After being sold into slavery, Joseph ended up as a servant in Potiphar's house in Egypt. Joseph was successful in his duties and had favor. After Potiphar's wife repeatedly tried to seduce Joseph to no avail, she accused him of attempted rape, which led to his imprisonment for ten years.

Joseph's Imprisonment and God's Purposes

- What three things does Dr. Thomas note about the temptation that Joseph faced?

  First of all, the temptation took place in the pathway of duty. Joseph faced great temptation, not when he was walking in disobedience, but precisely when he was walking in obedience to God. Second, the temptation was powerful. Potiphar's wife was in a position of great power, which would have made resisting the temptation quite difficult. Finally, the temptation was persistent. Joseph faced the temptation on a daily, ongoing basis.

- After Joseph reasoned through the temptation, how did he act decisively?

  Joseph fled from temptation. He did not reason with the sin itself and make any room for the temptation to take root. He immediately ran from the temptation in the fashion of Peter's words to "abstain from the passions of the flesh, which wage war against your soul" (1 Peter 2:11).

- According to Dr. Thomas, in what three ways was God with Joseph and working throughout his story?

  First, God was with Joseph in providentially preserving him. God preserved Joseph's life and transformed his character so that he would be prepared to carry out God's call on his life. Second, God was with Joseph in persistent temptation. Joseph was sustained by God to face persistent temptation and not yield to sin. Third, God was with Joseph for a purpose that Joseph did not yet know. God's providential plan was working throughout every step of Joseph's life so that Joseph would be used for God's purposes.

After the Video

- Consider what Joseph was like as a young boy and the transformation God wrought in him. How does God's work in Joseph throughout his life give hope to the believer today?

  Dr. Thomas draws the conclusion from the accounts in Genesis that Joseph was a somewhat self-focused, arrogant talebearer as a young boy. We see throughout the course of his life, however, that God transforms his character and produces a man who is faithful, flees temptation, and forgives great wrongs done against him. This should stir up immense hope in the hearts of believers in our own journeys of sanctification. It should also encourage us as we disciple others or walk alongside struggling children. We can gain encouragement that God will complete the good work that He has begun in His children (Phil. 1:6).

- For what purpose was God providentially preserving Joseph?

  In the immediate context, God was preserving Joseph for the purpose of saving the land of Israel from starvation during drought. But this had much grander implications. In Genesis 3:15, God promised that the seed of the woman would crush the serpent's head. In order for that to happen, God's promise to Abraham needed to be fulfilled. God promised Abraham that he would be a father of a multitude of people, thus necessitating the continuation of the people of Israel, the descendants of Abraham. God was with Joseph during every step of the journey, blessing him and causing him to find favor and success in order to carry out His plan of redemption.

- Dr. Thomas shares the following quote by John Owen: "Set faith at work on Christ for the killing of your sins and you will, in God's good providence, live to see your lust dead at your feet." How does the Christian practice this?

  This quote by John Owen succinctly summarizes the profound truths that Paul preached in Romans 5–8. As believers, we must preach the truths of the gospel to ourselves regularly so that we live in our identity as saints who are chosen by God and who are no longer under condemnation and slavery to sin. The power of sin has been defeated. Christ has broken sin's rule in our hearts and lives, and we are free to walk in obedience to Him. Practically, this is done by the ordinary means of grace—by filling our minds with God's Word, yielding to the Holy Spirit, repenting of sin, walking in forgiveness, and living in regular fellowship and community with the body of Christ.

REVIEW QUIZ

1. **A.**
   Joseph had a dream that his family would bow down to him. This was a reference to later in Joseph's life when he would be second in command in Egypt and would help his family and nation survive during a great famine.

2. **B.**
   John Bunyan was a Baptist preacher during the Puritan movement in England of the mid-seventeenth century. A law forbade unordained preachers to preach in established churches. Bunyan was not ordained, but he refused to stop preaching.

3. **D.**
   As Joseph faced temptation, he thought and reasoned quite carefully. He first reasoned that giving in to temptation would be a great misuse of the trust that Potiphar had placed in him. Second, Joseph reasoned that giving in to temptation would be a great offense against Potiphar as a husband. Finally, and most importantly, Joseph knew that it would be a great sin against God.

4. **A.**
In prison, Joseph discovered that God had given him the gift of interpreting dreams. He was able to interpret the jailer's dream and later Pharaoh's. This led to his release from prison, and he was elevated to a place of prominence.

5. **C.**
As Joseph was walking through the betrayal of his brothers, slavery, and imprisonment, he had no idea what God was doing. At the end of the story, however, he could look back and trace God's hand and clearly see His purposes in everything.

6. **B.**
God's presence is not removed in suffering. Rather, it is greatly manifest in the midst of suffering and trial, just as we see evidenced in Joseph's life. The end of Genesis records these words from Joseph to his brothers: "As for you, you meant evil against me, but God meant it for good" (Gen. 50:20). God is always working behind the scenes for His glory and the good of His people.

2

God's Grace to Samson

INTRODUCTION

How would we expect God to respond to a person who lives foolishly and licentiously? Would we expect that person to be met with God's judgment or grace? Samson was such a person. As a judge of Israel, he is remembered for his great strength, his love of riddles, his love of women, and his defeat of the Philistines. In this lesson, Dr. Thomas explores the life of Samson and God's abundant grace in the face of foolishness and self-dependence.

LEARNING GOALS

When you have finished this lesson, you should be able to:

- Explain the faltering faith of Samson in his foolishness
- Marvel at the glorious grip of God's grace

KEY IDEAS

- Samson lived in the period of the judges when every man did that which was right in his own eyes; Samson was no exception.
- God uses disasters and other difficulties as both punishment and purification.
- People must come to the end of themselves before they are ready to acknowledge that they are nothing without God.
- Israel needed deliverance; Jesus Christ is the perfect and final Deliverer.

REFLECTION & DISCUSSION QUESTIONS

Before the Video

What Do You Think?

Take a moment to answer the following questions. They will prepare you for the lecture.

- What comes to mind when you think about Samson and his story?

- Is God's grace dependent on our faith and performance?

Scripture Reading

> *And what more shall I say? For time would fail me to tell of Gideon, Barak, Samson, Jephthah, of David and Samuel and the prophets—who through faith conquered kingdoms, enforced justice, obtained promises, stopped the mouths of lions, quenched the power of fire, escaped the edge of the sword, were made strong out of weakness, became mighty in war, put foreign armies to flight.*
>
> —Hebrews 11:32–34

- How does this passage describe Samson?

During the Video

Answer the following questions while you watch the video. They will guide you through the lecture.

The Faltering Faith of a Foolish Man *0:00–14:37*

- What happens when you tune out the Holy Spirit?

- The period of the judges is known as a time when everyone did what was right in his own eyes. Was Samson any different? Why or why not?

- How did Samson handle temptation?

The Glorious Grip of a Gracious God *14:37–23:23*

- Toward the end of Samson's story when he is imprisoned by the Philistines, Dr. Thomas identifies a "but God" moment. What is this moment in the story?

- God heard Samson's prayer and gave him the strength to push against the pillars, bringing the temple crashing down on the Philistines and himself. Was this an act of punishment or purification?

- What does Dr. Thomas believe to be the primary lesson as we consider Samson?

After the Video

Answer the following questions after you have finished the lecture. They will help you identify and summarize the major points.

- Dr. Thomas describes some of the different judges as impressive, attractive, blunt, confused, and idiotic. Yet God used all these judges for various purposes according to His plan. What can this teach us about how we view people and make judgments?

  We can all think of someone whom we didn't expect to be used of God but who ended up being greatly used by Him. If you are in a group, have the members discuss an example of someone who, though the person perhaps didn't expect it, ended up serving the Lord faithfully.

- While we might not readily identify with Samson, John Milton pointed out that Samson is "the mirror of our fickle state." What did Milton mean, and how might you see yourself in this "mirror"?

  If you are in a group, have the members spend some time talking about how one comes to humility of heart. Ask: Why is the light of Scripture crucial for this process?

- What happens when a person trusts in his own strength? Why was Samson bound and blinded?

  If you are in a group, have the members share about the people in their lives that they are burdened to see come to the Lord. Ask: Do you ever struggle with giving up hope that God will save them? Why or why not?

PRAYER

Commit what you have learned from God's Word in this lesson to prayer.

- Praise God for His glorious and gracious grip on our lives.
- Confess where you've been tempted to give up on a person, losing hope that God can still reach his or her heart.
- Thank God for His preserving grace in your own life.
- Ask God to grow your understanding of His nature and character, that you might better worship Him.

REVIEW QUIZ

Use these multiple-choice questions to measure what you learned from this lesson.

1. Within the Jewish tradition, Samson is viewed as a righteous man.
   a. True
   b. False

2. According to Dr. Thomas, what one job did Samson have to do?
   a. Maintain Nazirite vows
   b. Kill the Philistines
   c. Rescue Delilah
   d. Rescue Israel

3. Why did the Philistines want to kill Samson?
   a. Samson was with Delilah.
   b. Samson destroyed their crops.
   c. Samson threatened to kill them.
   d. Samson was dedicated to being a Nazirite.

4. Which of the following was *not* a part of the Nazirite vows?
   a. Not touching alcohol
   b. Not cutting one's hair
   c. Not marrying a Philistine
   d. Keeping away from defilement

5. What was the physical expression of Samson's losing his strength and the presence of God?
   a. The cutting of his hair
   b. Grinding flour on a mill
   c. The act of carrying the city gates
   d. Blindness at the hands of the Philistines

6. What was the ultimate purpose of the judges, prophets, kings, and priests in Israel?
   a. To rule perfectly
   b. To offer forgiveness of sins
   c. To point to the perfect Lord Jesus
   d. To bring judgment on God's people

Answer Key—God's Grace to Samson

REFLECTION & DISCUSSION QUESTIONS

Before the Video

What Do You Think?

These are personal questions. The answers should be based on your own knowledge and experience.

Scripture Reading

- How does this passage describe Samson?

  Samson is named among other judges, kings, and prophets here in Hebrews 11. While he is a man of many shortcomings, he's remembered in this passage for his faith. This passage lists ways that men in these various roles were faithful to carry out their God-ordained purposes. Samson's name and accomplishments listed here are a reminder that God can use even the faintest faith for His purposes and His glory and that it is never too late. Samson was faithful because God is faithful.

During the Video

The Faltering Faith of a Foolish Man

- What happens when you tune out the Holy Spirit?

  When you tune out the Holy Spirit, you're saying that you know best. But Proverbs 28:26 declares, "Whoever trusts in his own mind is a fool." We are foolish when we are tuned in to ourselves rather than the Holy Spirit because this makes us unaware of surrounding dangers. Not only do you put yourself in danger, but you also put others in danger.

- The period of the judges is known as a time when everyone did what was right in his own eyes. Was Samson any different? Why or why not?

  Samson was no different from his culture for the majority of his life; nor was he different in the majority of the decisions he made. He was a man who did what was right in his own eyes, giving in to addictions, sex, and erratic and foolish behavior. His focus was on pleasing himself rather than pleasing God.

- How did Samson handle temptation?

  Rather than running from temptation as we saw Joseph do, Samson walked right into it. He made no efforts whatsoever to flee or avoid temptation. Instead, he flirted with it and sees how close he could get to it. This attitude toward sin is consistent with Samson's overall attitude of superficiality and not taking life seriously.

The Glorious Grip of a Gracious God

- Toward the end of Samson's story when he is imprisoned by the Philistines, Dr. Thomas identifies a "but God" moment. What is this moment in the story?

  Even in Samson's pride and foolishness, God didn't cease being faithful. At the Philistine gathering, Samson prayed for the first and only recorded time. God stirred the embers of faith and answered Samson's prayer for strength to defeat the Philistines. God is always faithful to His people and His promises. As Ephesians 2:4 states, we were dead in our sins, "but God" displayed His mercy and made us alive in Christ.

- God heard Samson's prayer and gave him the strength to push against the pillars, bringing the temple crashing down on the Philistines and himself. Was this an act of punishment or purification?

  We must be careful in calling disasters and suffering acts of judgment. Yet there are times when God is clearly bringing forth judgment. Dr. Thomas points out that the same circumstances can be punitive for one while being purifying for another. Such is the case in this instance. For Samson, God used his imprisonment and trial as a final act of purification. For the Philistines, however, it was a punitive act of judgment.

- What does Dr. Thomas believe to be the primary lesson as we consider Samson?

  According to Dr. Thomas, the story of Samson is a story of how not to live our lives. Dr. Thomas cautions us not to waste our lives and the time that God has given us. Although Samson did fulfill his purpose in the end, he squandered his whole life up until that point. He could have had more opportunities to be faithful to the Lord.

After the Video

- Dr. Thomas describes some of the different judges as impressive, attractive, blunt, confused, and idiotic. Yet God used all these judges for various purposes according to His plan. What can this teach us about how we view people and make judgments?

  According to Isaiah 55:8, God's ways are not our ways. In 1 Samuel, we find that God looks on the heart while man looks on outward appearances. These are helpful reminders as we consider people and their contributions to the kingdom of God. He uses a variety of people with unique personalities and gifts to bring about His purposes, and He is sovereign, even over foolishness. God is committed to transforming His people and will accomplish this transformation for His glory and our good.

- While we might not readily identify with Samson, John Milton pointed out that Samson is "the mirror of our fickle state." What did Milton mean, and how might you see yourself in this "mirror"?

We would probably all agree that Samson is not someone we would want to be like. When Milton says, "He is the mirror of our fickle state," that flies in the face of our pride. We might be tempted to think, "No, not me." If we humble ourselves, however, we find more in common with Samson than we might think. Samson's main problem was pride. He thought too highly of himself and did what was right in his own eyes rather than pursuing what was right and pleasing to the Lord. While our areas of pride and sin might not be as overt as Samson's, we all have subtle areas of sin lurking in our hearts. Sin blinds us all. If we give in, we will lose sight of reality just as Samson did.

- What happens when a person trusts in his own strength? Why was Samson bound and blinded?

  Samson is a prime example of what happens when a person trusts in his own strength. Proverbs 16:18 is an apt description: "Pride goes before destruction, and a haughty spirit before a fall." Samson was so self-reliant that he didn't even know when the presence of the Lord departed from him and that he no longer possessed supernatural strength. Ironically, when Samson was physically blinded, his spiritual eyes were opened to see the true state of his soul and his desperate need for God. Dr. Thomas observes, "God had to bind him and blind him to make him acknowledge that without God we are nothing."

REVIEW QUIZ

1. **B.**
   In the Jewish tradition, Samson is considered an unrighteous man. He's a man who is not even worthy to be read about on Shabbat and holy days. His story is found to be unhelpful and uninspiring.
2. **D.**
   Samson was tasked by God with one job: to rescue Israel. While Samson wasted the majority of his life on his own pleasures, he did fulfill his duty and is even named among the faithful in Hebrews 11.
3. **B.**
   In his anger over losing his wife in a game of riddles, Samson tied foxes' tails together, set the tails on fire, and set the foxes to run wild through the crops. Thus, the crops of the Philistines were destroyed.
4. **C.**
   The Nazirite vow included not touching alcohol, not cutting one's hair, and not touching anything defiling. Samson managed to break all these vows throughout his life.
5. **A.**
   When Samson shared with Delilah that the secret of his strength was in his hair, she cut his hair and his strength left him without his knowledge. This also represented God's withdrawing His presence from Samson.

6. **C.**

   Israel needed deliverance, but the deliverance provided through judges and kings was only partial. The final Deliverer is none other than Jesus Christ. He is the perfect Judge, King, Prophet, and Priest. All those who served in these roles were merely imperfect shadows of the perfect One.

3

God's Sovereignty with Micaiah

INTRODUCTION

Imagine being in battle, closing your eyes, and taking a random shot toward the battlefield with your bow and arrow. Then imagine learning that your arrow had struck and killed the king. This story sounds like one of great chance or luck out of an imaginary storybook, but it is a story from God's Word that demonstrates His precise sovereignty. In this lesson, Dr. Thomas looks at the sovereignty of God in the story of the prophet Micaiah and King Ahab.

LEARNING GOALS

When you have finished this lesson, you should be able to:

- Identify areas of God's sovereignty
- Understand the importance of God's rule over evil

KEY IDEAS

- God is sovereign over everything; His dominion is total.
- God always acts to fulfill His purposes.
- God is a covenant-keeping God; He reigns over the smallest details to fulfill His promises.

REFLECTION & DISCUSSION QUESTIONS

Before the Video

What Do You Think?

Take a moment to answer the following questions. They will prepare you for the lecture.

- What do you know about the prophet Micaiah?

- Do you believe that God is sovereign over everything in your life? How ought this truth to affect your day-to-day life?

Scripture Reading

Then Job answered the Lord *and said: "I know that you can do all things, and that no purpose of yours can be thwarted."*

—Job 42:1–2

- What made Job able to acknowledge God's sovereignty?

During the Video

Answer the following questions while you watch the video. They will guide you through the lecture.

God Is Sovereign *0:00–12:14*

- Who was Micaiah?
- What is providence, and what does this doctrine help to explain?
- What does the author of Chronicles want to communicate in this story?

The Details of God's Sovereignty *12:14–23:10*

- According to Dr. Thomas, believing and cherishing what will change a person's life?
- What are the four lessons that Dr. Thomas draws from this account?
- In being sovereign over Ahab's death, what was God also sovereign over?

After the Video

Answer the following questions after you have finished the lecture. They will help you identify and summarize the major points.

- Why can the believer find comfort and rest in the sovereignty of God?

  If you are in a group, have the members discuss a time when they have found comfort in a situation because they were able to rest in God's sovereignty.

- What difficult statement in 2 Chronicles 18:22 does Dr. Thomas address, and why is it difficult?

  If you are in a group, have the members share whether this is a difficult statement for them personally. Ask: How have you wrestled with this issue, and what Scripture passages have been helpful for you?

- According to Charles Spurgeon, what is the problem with the language of permission when it comes to God's sovereignty?

  If you are in a group, have the members discuss what they think about Spurgeon's ideas of God's sovereignty over evil. To add to the discussion, have them read the account of God and Satan's dialogue in Job 1–2, paying special attention to the language used in 1:9–12 and 2:3–7.

PRAYER

Commit what you have learned from God's Word in this lesson to prayer.

- Praise God that He is a God of the details.
- Confess any areas where you have questioned God's purposes from a heart of pride, thinking your own ways were best.
- Thank God for His purposes that always come from His wise, good, and loving heart.
- Ask God to help you trust Him when you can't understand His purposes.

REVIEW QUIZ

Use these multiple-choice questions to measure what you learned from this lesson.

1. How was King Ahab killed?
   a. By the spear of Ahab's chariot driver
   b. By the hand of the wicked Jezebel
   c. By the arrow of a random man
   d. By Micaiah as God's judgment

2. Why was Micaiah imprisoned?
   a. He sided with King Jehoshaphat.
   b. He refused to prophesy about Ahab.
   c. He prophesied that Ahab would be killed.
   d. He made his hatred of Ahab known to all.

3. What is *open theism*?
   a. The idea that God plans the big things but leaves the details to get sorted out
   b. The belief that God's dominion is total, reaching over everything big and small
   c. The belief that God has no control over people and circumstances whatsoever
   d. The idea that God orchestrates the details without an overarching plan and end goal

4. God is sovereign over random and chaotic events—even evil.
   a. True
   b. False

5. What important event did Peter address in Acts 2 that pertains to this lesson?
   a. The birth of Christ
   b. The crucifixion of Christ
   c. The burial of Christ
   d. The resurrection of Christ

6. What are the two lessons that we can see in the death of Ahab?
   a. Perseverance and promises
   b. Power and providence
   c. Penance and penalty
   d. Prayer and patience

Answer Key—God's Sovereignty in Micaiah

REFLECTION & DISCUSSION QUESTIONS

Before the Video

What Do You Think?

These are personal questions. The answers should be based on your own knowledge and experience.

Scripture Reading

- What made Job able to acknowledge God's sovereignty?

  The lesson came through fiery trial. Job was able to acknowledge God's sovereignty after facing trials and coming face-to-face with who God is. At the end of Job's suffering and trials, he acknowledged his own humanity, limitations, and weakness; he acknowledged God's absolute control over everything. He understood that God is sovereign, that what He wills happens, and that nothing can come against it.

During the Video

God Is Sovereign

- Who was Micaiah?

  We read about Micaiah in 2 Chronicles 18. He was a prophet during the rule of Jehoshaphat over the southern kingdom of Judah and of Ahab over the northern kingdom of Israel. These kings were forming a marriage alliance and agreed to go to war together to seal the alliance.

- What is providence, and what does this doctrine help to explain?

  Providence is the doctrine that nothing happens without God's willing it to happen. He wills it to happen before it happens and in the way it will happen. Another name for this doctrine is the sovereignty of God. Providence explains the so-called random happenstances in life, which unbelievers commonly think of as luck.

- What does the author of Chronicles want to communicate in this story?

  The author is trying to communicate that God is sovereign and keeps His covenant. God's covenant and promises are sure. Nothing can thwart the hand of God. The books of 1 and 2 Chronicles teach us that God was preserving the godly line of King David according to His covenant with David (see 2 Sam. 7).

The Details of God's Sovereignty

- According to Dr. Thomas, believing and cherishing what will change a person's life?

  Dr. Thomas quoted Heidelberg Catechism 27. The answer to this question focuses on the character of God—He is almighty, omnipresent, and powerful. He governs all things so that both good and bad come through the Father's hand. It is this truth that Dr. Thomas says will change a person's life when he or she believes and cherishes it.

- What are the four lessons that Dr. Thomas draws from this account?

  The primary lesson of this account from Scripture is that God is sovereign—He rules and reigns over all. Yet Dr. Thomas doesn't leave the lesson there. It's important to understand the vastness and the depth of God's sovereignty. When we say that nothing is outside His sovereign will, we mean nothing. *God is in the things we might be tempted to question most—seemingly chance events, evil, and both life and death.*

- In being sovereign over Ahab's death, what was God also sovereign over?

  Through Ahab's death, God ensured the final outcome, which was the survival of the house of David in Jerusalem. Ahab's death was not only about one man's appointed death and judgment; God was weaving together a greater story and making sure to destroy the alliance between Jehoshaphat and Ahab to preserve David's line. God used Ahab's death to accomplish His purpose.

After the Video

- Why can the believer find comfort and rest in the sovereignty of God?

  Dr. Thomas describes the total sovereignty of God as an understanding that every detail of the future is ordered by God. Nothing in the past, present, or future is outside His dominion. Not only do His attributes of omnipotence and omniscience come into play here, but so do His attributes of love, wisdom, and goodness. God decrees what will happen, without exception, for the good of those who love Him. His attributes work together in perfect harmony so that believers can rest fully secure with their trust placed fully in a God who is in control and loves them. God has a plan and a purpose; it will not be thwarted.

- What difficult statement in 2 Chronicles 18:22 does Dr. Thomas address, and why is it difficult?

  According to 2 Chronicles 18:22, God "put a lying spirit in the mouth" of Ahab's prophets. That is a difficult statement because it seems to say that God is the author of evil. Many people struggle with the problem of evil and ask, "How could a good, loving God allow evil?" As Dr. Thomas points out, God doesn't permit evil "willy-nilly." God always works according to His purposes and according to His character.

- According to Charles Spurgeon, what is the problem with the language of permission when it comes to God's sovereignty?

  Spurgeon had a problem with using the language of permission when it comes to how God does things. According to Spurgeon, this reduces everything to fatalism or stoicism. Spurgeon said that the difference between fate and providence is that fate has no end purpose. Providence says that God ordains everything, but all this must be ordained by God's wisdom according to the end purpose that He is working out. God doesn't act just to act; He acts to bring about His specific, wise, good, and glorious plan.

REVIEW QUIZ

1. **C.**
   According to 2 Chronicles 18:33, "a certain man drew his bow at random and struck the king of Israel between the scale armor and the breastplate." This unnamed man may have shot his arrow at random, but God placed the man and his arrow precisely where they would accomplish His will.

2. **C.**
   Ahab was used to being told what he wanted to hear. When he asked for a prophet, he was displeased to find that it was Micaiah, who no longer told Ahab what he wanted to hear. When Micaiah prophesied that Ahab would be killed in battle and it came true, Micaiah was put in prison.

3. **A.**
   Open theism *is the idea that the future is open because God plans the big things and leaves the small details to get sorted out by themselves. While not quite as popular now, this was a popular view in the late twentieth and early twenty-first centuries.*

4. **A.**
   God is sovereign over all events, even the ones that seem to be random, chaotic, or evil. According to Matthew 10:29, a sparrow does not even fall to the ground apart from God's will. As the classic hymn says, "His eye is on the sparrow, and I know He watches me." Knowing that God is over every event—great and small—should cause us to worship.

5. **B.**
   Peter spoke about the crucifixion of Christ in Acts 2 as he addressed the people in Jerusalem. The significance of this passage is that Peter asserted that Christ was crucified at the hands of wicked men but that this was done "according to the definite plan and foreknowledge of God" (Acts 2:23). Without God's ordaining this great act of evil, we would have no gospel.

6. **D.**
As a result of Ahab's death, Jehoshaphat learned to lean on the Lord. Out of fear, he set his face upon the Lord and prayed in faith. Patience can also be learned from the death of Ahab. Everything looked to be a mess in the life of Micaiah, but in the prophet's patiently waiting until the end, God was shown to be in control in his prophecy's being fulfilled.

4

God's Persistence with Jonah

INTRODUCTION

The story of "Jonah and the whale" is a tale that most children are taught in Sunday school. Most of us probably have flannelgraph images in our minds and can easily recount the events that happened. Yet many of us might have missed the profound work that God was doing and the incredible depths of His mercy and grace. In this lesson, Dr. Thomas explains the disobedience of Jonah and his unconventional "imprisonment" that leads to valuable lessons for both Jonah and us.

LEARNING GOALS

When you have finished this lesson, you should be able to:

- Summarize the story of Jonah
- Describe the lessons Jonah learned in the belly of the great fish
- Apply Jonah's lessons to your own heart and life

KEY IDEAS

- The presence of God cannot be escaped, and we cannot flee from His gaze.
- God will go to great lengths to reveal and capture a person's heart.
- A robust vocabulary of prayer is learned from God's Word.

REFLECTION & DISCUSSION QUESTIONS

Before the Video

What Do You Think?

Take a moment to answer the following questions. They will prepare you for the lecture.

- How would you explain the story of Jonah to someone unfamiliar with it?

- Put yourself in Jonah's shoes. How do you think you would have responded to God's call?

Scripture Reading

> *I called out to the LORD, out of my distress, and he answered me; out of the belly of Sheol I cried, and you heard my voice.*
>
> —Jonah 2:2

- According to this verse, why should we be motivated to pray?

During the Video

Answer the following questions while you watch the video. They will guide you through the lecture.

Jonah's Disobedience and "Imprisonment" *0:00–9:52*

- How do we know that these events really happened and are not just a story or allegory?
- According to Sinclair Ferguson, where was the deep work of God done in this story?

Jonah's Lessons *9:52–23:05*

- What is the first lesson that Jonah learned about himself, and how do we know this?
- What is the second lesson that Jonah learned in the belly of the fish?
- What is the final lesson that Jonah learned while "imprisoned" in the fish's belly?

After the Video

Answer the following questions after you have finished the lecture. They will help you identify and summarize the major points.

- What is the meaning and significance of Jonah's fleeing from the "presence" of God?

  While in our human relationships we often physically avoid eye contact and turn our backs when we feel shame, we don't literally do this with God. If you are in a group, have the members discuss the various ways that we do attempt to hide or flee from God's presence. Ask: What should we do instead in these moments?

- What was argued is the purpose of the Psalms?

  If you are in a group, have the members discuss ways that they might use the Psalms for prayer. Then have them spend some time praying through a psalm together. Consider Psalm 33 or 34 as a good starting place.

- How can a person face suffering with gratitude and without complaint?

  If you are in a group, have the members discuss how God has brought them through similar seasons and the lessons that He taught them.

PRAYER

Commit what you have learned from God's Word in this lesson to prayer.

- Praise God for His marvelous grace that reaches to our lowest depths.
- Confess areas of disobedience that you've perhaps tried to hide.
- Thank God for the lessons in His Word for us that others have previously learned.
- Ask God to teach you to pray, believing that He hears you and answers you.

REVIEW QUIZ

Use these multiple-choice questions to measure what you learned from this lesson.

1. Why didn't Jonah like the Ninevites?
   a. They had taken him captive.
   b. They were hypocritical people.
   c. They were pagan enemies of Israel.
   d. They sent him on a ship to Tarshish.

2. According to Dr. Thomas, what was Jonah's central problem?
   a. Himself
   b. The Ninevites
   c. God's instructions
   d. Money for the journey

3. Why was there a storm at sea on Jonah's journey to Tarshish?
   a. It was God's judgment on the sailors for taking Jonah on board.
   b. It was God's judgment on Jonah for his poor decision-making.
   c. Such storms were a common occurrence during this season.
   d. It was God's means to get the fish to the right place to swallow Jonah.

4. How long was Jonah in the belly of the fish?
   a. Two days and two nights
   b. Two days and three nights
   c. Three days and two nights
   d. Three days and three nights

5. As Jonah is in the belly of the fish, he longs most to be released from the belly of the fish.
   a. True
   b. False

6. According to Dr. Thomas, what is the sad reality for Jonah and often us, too?
   a. God didn't pursue the sailors, and He doesn't pursue everyone in our lives.
   b. Jonah wasted time on his voyage to Tarshish, and we often waste time ourselves.
   c. Sin doesn't affect only us. Jonah's sin affected others, and our sin affects others, too.
   d. It takes great extremes to wake us up to the reality of who God is and the truth of the gospel.

Answer Key— God's Persistence with Jonah

REFLECTION & DISCUSSION QUESTIONS

Before the Video

What Do You Think?

These are personal questions. The answers should be based on your own knowledge and experience.

Scripture Reading

- According to this verse, why should we be motivated to pray?

  This verse shows us Jonah's response to being within the belly of the fish. Jonah cried out in desperation to God, and God heard him. The verse underscores this twice in the lines "he answered me" and "you heard my voice." What greater motivation should there be for us to pray? The God of the universe hears us. The depth of our heart and circumstances are not at too great a distance to silence our cries in God's ears.

During the Video

Jonah's Disobedience and "Imprisonment"

- How do we know that these events really happened and are not just a story or allegory?

  Jesus referenced this account in Matthew 12 when the scribes and Pharisees asked Him for a sign. Jesus offered them the sign of Jonah, explaining that Jonah "was three days and three nights in the belly of the great fish" and "so will the Son of Man be three days and three nights in the heart of the earth" (v. 40). Jesus spoke of Jonah's experience as a historical event.

- According to Sinclair Ferguson, where was the deep work of God done in this story?

  Dr. Ferguson said, "The deeper work of God took place not in the belly of the whale but in Jonah's heart." While Jonah was indeed deep in the belly of a great fish, the main focus of the story is not that fact but the deep work that God began in Jonah's heart. Often, people get sidetracked by questions about how Jonah would have survived, but this is missing the point. The point is the heart of Jonah and not the nature of these extraordinary events.

Jonah's Lessons

- What is the first lesson that Jonah learned about himself, and how do we know this?

Jonah's response after being swallowed by the fish was to pray. In his prayer, Jonah said, "Those who pay regard to vain idols forsake their hope of steadfast love" (2:8). This refers to a turning away from covenant love. Therefore, Jonah realized that he was a sinner. In God's great mercy, He sent the fish to swallow Jonah so that Jonah could realize his sin and cry out to God.

- What is the second lesson that Jonah learned in the belly of the fish?

  Jonah learned the great lengths to which God will go to pursue and find His own. God is sovereign and omnipresent. Jonah could not outrun God even though he tried in his rebellion to do so. In Jonah's prayer, he described his state as being in Sheol, in the realm of the dead. Nowhere is too far away for God's presence and the merciful reach of His hand.

- What is the final lesson that Jonah learned while "imprisoned" in the fish's belly?

  Jonah rediscovered grace while in the fish's belly. Jonah's prayer indicates that God was at work in his heart reviving his worship, prayer, and consecration. According to Dr. Thomas, Jonah's offer of thanksgiving and sacrifice, combined with his acknowledgment that he would pay his vow, is an indication that a work of grace had begun in his heart. Only when someone understands grace deeply is that person willing to pay vows, live for the Lord, and consecrate himself or herself to Him.

After the Video

- What is the meaning and significance of Jonah's fleeing from the "presence" of God?

  The Hebrew word for "presence" is also the word for "face." Jonah's attempt at fleeing from the presence of God carried the idea of avoiding eye contact and turning one's back. Jonah even took it a step further when he tried to literally run away from God. Jonah, however, was not the only one who went to such measures. This goes all the way back to Adam and Eve in the garden of Eden. They tried to hide from God because they were too ashamed of their sin to look at Him in His face. Because of their sin, they didn't want to make eye contact. Jonah, along with Adam and Eve, was deceived; he could not hide from God's gaze.

- What was argued is the purpose of the Psalms?

  The Psalms are the prayers of God's people, and for many years, the church has borrowed language from the Psalms to help form prayers. The Psalms cover almost every human emotion we can experience—hurt, anger, jealousy, confusion, lament, joy, contentment, and so on. When the child of God has great feelings but doesn't know what words to use, the Psalms provide "the vocabulary of prayer," as Dr. Thomas says.

- How can a person face suffering with gratitude and without complaint?

  Anne Steele wrote: "Father, whate'er of earthly bliss Thy sovereign will denies, accepted at Thy throne of grace, let this petition rise. Give me a calm, a thankful heart, from every murmur free; the blessings of Thy grace impart, and make me live for Thee." We do not prepare ourselves for the big trials of life through one big preparation, like cramming for a final exam. We prepare ourselves by cultivating hearts of humility, dependence, and trust through all the ordinary moments of life and the "little" trials that come day in and day out. A heart that responds to such suffering and disappointment in this way is a heart that has steadfastly been pursuing the Lord, His Word, fellowship with the saints, and the ordinary means of grace. A heart that understands one's position before God as being a sinner and utterly dependent on God's mercy and grace is the heart that will then surrender when all is stripped away.

REVIEW QUIZ

1. **C.**
   Jonah did not like the Ninevites because they were pagans. In addition, they were Israel's enemies and had seized expansion and political opportunities. Jonah's hatred of the Ninevites was a form of racial despising.

2. **A.**
   The book of Jonah opens with God's command for Jonah to go to Nineveh and Jonah's attempt "to go . . . to Tarshish, away from the presence of the LORD" (1:3). The central problem here is Jonah.

3. **B.**
   The storm was God's means of judging Jonah. Immediately, Jonah knew this without any question. He made an offer for the sailors to throw him into the sea, knowing that God's wrath would be appeased and that the men would be saved.

4. **D.**
   According to Jonah 1:17, the fish was appointed by the Lord to swallow Jonah, and he remained in the fish's belly for three days and three nights. This is significant because Jesus referred to this when He indicated that He would be buried for three days and three nights (Matt. 12:38–41).

5. **B.**
   The language of the Psalms, which was probably very familiar to Jonah, came to the surface as he cried out to God from the fish's belly. Jonah longed to be back in the temple; he longed to experience God's steadfast love and covenant mercies.

6. **D.**
   Often, in our stubbornness and pride, we are more like Jonah than we might wish to think. Sometimes it takes a lot to get our attention and wake us up, just as it did with Jonah. Thankfully, God is kind and merciful.

5

God's Dark Providence & Jeremiah

INTRODUCTION

Israel went through numerous dark times as a nation as God called the people to repentance for their sin and rebellion. Jeremiah was a prophet in one of these dark periods of Israel's history, and he faced great distress as he faithfully preached to God's people. In this lesson, Dr. Thomas explains the context of Jeremiah 20, why Jeremiah was imprisoned for a brief period, and how we can find comfort even in the seemingly dark passages of Scripture.

LEARNING GOALS

When you have finished this lesson, you should be able to:

- Describe the ministry of Jeremiah
- Better understand sin and suffering in God's providence
- Understand the language and heart of lament in Scripture and how it is relevant to us today
- Identify passages of Scripture to turn to for comfort in distress

KEY IDEAS

- As humans, we suffer at different times with varying levels of discouragement, pain, and hopelessness.
- God uses our weakness to accomplish His purposes for His glory and our good.

REFLECTION & DISCUSSION QUESTIONS

Before the Video

What Do You Think?

Take a moment to answer the following questions. They will prepare you for the lecture.

- What do you currently know about Jeremiah?

- Think of a time that you were in deep despair. How did you respond, and how did you find comfort?

Scripture Reading

> *For you formed my inward parts; you knitted me together in my mother's womb. . . . My frame was not hidden from you, when I was being made in secret, intricately woven in the depths of the earth. Your eyes saw my unformed substance; in your book were written, every one of them, the days that were formed for me, when as yet there was none of them.*
>
> —Psalm 139:13, 15–16

- How does this passage give hope to a person who is suffering?

During the Video

Answer the following questions while you watch the video. They will guide you through the lecture.

Jeremiah's Ministry and the Outcome *0:00–11:42*

- Who was Jeremiah?

- What was Jeremiah's message to the people of Judah, and how did they respond?

- Why was Jeremiah put in the stocks?

How Jeremiah Responded to God's Dark Providence *11:42–23:39*

- Why was Jeremiah in pain, feeling hopeless?

- How does Dr. Thomas explain the question whether Job's or Jeremiah's suffering was due to his sin?

- When did Jesus experience profound "heaviness"?

After the Video

Answer the following questions after you have finished the lecture. They will help you identify and summarize the major points.

- Dr. Thomas makes a distinction between the public Jeremiah and the private Jeremiah. Typically, we talk about the importance of being the same person in public and private. What is Dr. Thomas trying to point out here?

  If you are in a group, have the members discuss ways that they seek to refresh their souls in the Lord during wearying times or times of heavy ministry and burdens.

- Dr. Thomas says that the Bible is refreshing and relevant to the moments and experiences that we face today. How is that true as we think of Job and Jeremiah?

  If you are in a group, have the members discuss some Scripture passages that they turn to in their own times of darkness of soul. If time permits, have them read some of the passages aloud together.

- What kind of vessels does God use to do His work and why? Where would you go in Scripture to demonstrate this idea?

  If you are in a group, have the members discuss a time when they saw God show up and use them in their weakness.

PRAYER

Commit what you have learned from God's Word in this lesson to prayer.

- Praise God that He is a God of hope and peace.
- Confess any ways that you have been quick to counsel like Job's friends and accuse of sin instead of offering comfort and hope.
- Thank God for giving you the Scriptures to rehearse His character, promises, and faithfulness.
- Ask God to deepen your understanding of His Word so that you may find hope in seasons of darkness of soul.

REVIEW QUIZ

Use these multiple-choice questions to measure what you learned from this lesson.

1. What is Jeremiah often called and known as?
   a. "The Harsh Prophet"
   b. "The Weeping Prophet"
   c. "The Rejoicing Prophet"
   d. "The Compassionate Prophet"

2. Although Jeremiah was a prophet during a dark time, who was one of the great kings during Jeremiah's period of ministry?
   a. Josiah
   b. Pashhur
   c. Heman
   d. Zedekiah

3. How is the book of Jeremiah organized?
   a. Thematically
   b. Systematically
   c. Chronologically
   d. Argumentatively

4. Jeremiah's words of lament and woe were almost identical to whose words?
   a. Habakkuk
   b. Ezekiel
   c. Isaiah
   d. Job

5. Passages such as Jeremiah 20 add validity to the inspiration and inerrancy of Scripture.
   a. True
   b. False

6. Who was given to depression and tried to take his own life?
   a. John Newton
   b. Michelangelo
   c. William Cowper
   d. Adoniram Judson

Answer Key—God's Dark Providence & Jeremiah

REFLECTION & DISCUSSION QUESTIONS

Before the Video

What Do You Think?

These are personal questions. The answers should be based on your own knowledge and experience.

Scripture Reading

- How does this passage give hope to a person who is suffering?

  This passage is often quoted in matters concerning the unborn. But if we are honest, most of us have wondered about the purpose of our lives or even struggled, just like Job and Jeremiah, with wishing that we had never been born. This psalm reminds us that God formed us in the womb. The psalmist uses words such as "knitted" and "woven." These words denote personal, detailed craftsmanship. Even in our darkest times, we can trust our Creator. He is intimately acquainted with us and has specific purposes for our lives.

During the Video

Jeremiah's Ministry and the Outcome

- Who was Jeremiah?

  Jeremiah was a prophet for many years during the reign of several kings, including Zedekiah. The fall of Judah to the Babylonians occurred during this time from 597 to 587 BC. Jeremiah was a prophet during a very dark time, tasked with preaching repentance to a people who would not listen.

- What was Jeremiah's message to the people of Judah, and how did they respond?

  Jeremiah was tasked by God with telling the people of Judah that war and destruction were coming. Judah would lose the war to Babylon, which was a powerful nation at that time. Jeremiah's message to the people was to surrender, and the people saw him as a traitor and hated him for it.

- Why was Jeremiah put in the stocks?

  In Jeremiah 20, Jeremiah was in the temple, preaching. He was warning the people that they were sinners and had displeased God. Because of this, God's judgment was coming upon them through the Babylonians. Jeremiah urged them to repent. Pashhur, who was part of the temple police on the lookout for heresy, didn't like this, arrested Jeremiah, and put him in the stocks.

How Jeremiah Responded to God's Dark Providence

- Why was Jeremiah in pain, feeling hopeless?

  Jeremiah's mission from God was to preach a message to people who were stubborn and rebellious and would not listen. The people did not have ears to hear or eyes to see the truth that Jeremiah was proclaiming. Imagine laboring in ministry and seeing no converts, not one person walking in repentance. That was Jeremiah's plight.

- How does Dr. Thomas explain the question whether Job's or Jeremiah's suffering was due to his sin?

  According to Dr. Thomas, it's not a matter of whether Job and Jeremiah had sin in their lives. The answer to that question is an obvious yes because we all have sin in our lives. Dr. Thomas further explains that there's no record of God's chastising them for sin. The passages that Job and Jeremiah wrote were cries from the depths of their souls. They were hurting and broken and did exactly what they ought to have done—cry out to God.

- When did Jesus experience profound "heaviness"?

  Jesus experienced profound heaviness in the garden of Gethsemane before His arrest and crucifixion. Jesus pleaded with God the Father to provide a way out of the suffering that He was about to go through. If Jesus, the Son of God, experienced heaviness of soul and cried out to the Father, how much more should we cry out to our heavenly Father?

After the Video

- Dr. Thomas makes a distinction between the public Jeremiah and the private Jeremiah. Typically, we talk about the importance of being the same person in public and private. What is Dr. Thomas trying to point out here?

  The public ministry of Jeremiah was a deep, heavy one. He was preaching judgment to people who would not listen and repent, a wearying and burdensome task. Dr. Thomas emphasizes Jeremiah's humanity. He was a man who could handle only so much ministry. He reached a point where his soul could take it no longer, and he burst out in cries to the Lord. Jeremiah was sorrowful and needed his own heart ministered to. He needed to cry out in both worship and lament.

- Dr. Thomas says that the Bible is refreshing and relevant to the moments and experiences that we face today. How is that true as we think of Job and Jeremiah?

  When we read in Scripture that men such as Job and Jeremiah questioned their own lives and wished that they had never been born, it makes the Bible and those characters relatable. Often in the Christian life, we feel unique or as though something is wrong with us when we wrestle with God and our various circumstances. It's refreshing to find that there are others just like us. We are not alone; others have gone before us and come out on the other side of suffering. As we meditate on these stories and characters, it brings relevance and refreshment to our own hearts.

- What kind of vessels does God use to do His work and why? Where would you go in Scripture to demonstrate this idea?

  God uses broken vessels to do His work. Paul wrote the following in 2 Corinthians 4:7: "But we have this treasure in jars of clay, to show that the surpassing power belongs to God and not to us." Elsewhere, this was God's answer to Paul when he asked for the thorn in his flesh to be removed: "My grace is sufficient for you, for my power is made perfect in weakness." In response, Paul said, "Therefore I will boast all the more gladly of my weaknesses, so that the power of Christ may rest upon me" (2 Cor. 12:9). It is precisely through our weakness that God accomplishes His work and gets the glory. If we were strong, we could claim the glory for ourselves. This way, God gets the glory, and all the boasting is in Him alone.

REVIEW QUIZ

1. **B.**
   Jeremiah has been called "the Weeping Prophet" because of his difficult and dark ministry of preaching repentance to a people who would not repent. Michelangelo painted Jeremiah, and his depiction of the prophet conveys the sadness of his ministry.

2. **A.**
   Josiah was one of the great kings of Israel. He rediscovered the book of Deuteronomy and brought reform to Jerusalem. But he was killed in battle by the Egyptians, who were later defeated by the Babylonians.

3. **A.**
   The book of Jeremiah must be read and understood as a book that is thematic. The narrative is not chronological, which is important to know if one is to accurately study this book.

4. **D.**
   In Job 3, Job had penned words similar to Jeremiah's after Job's loss of his children, his wealth, and his wife's respect. Job questioned why God had even let him be born, since it would have been better to have not known life than to have life with such tremendous suffering.

5. **A.**
   Passages such as this show real, honest men and women of God. This demonstrates the inspiration of Scripture because if mere humans were writing the Bible, they

would have edited out scenes such as these to make it more attractive and appealing. The fact that people in Scripture are messy points to its divine inspiration.

6. **C.**
William Cowper was so given to depression that he tried to take his own life five times. He lived next door to John Newton, who was a tremendous encouragement and counselor. As a result of Cowper's struggles, he learned incredible lessons and penned beautiful truths that are still enjoyed today.

6

God's Courage to Daniel

INTRODUCTION

Daniel and the lions' den is a story that many of us have heard since childhood. We've been taught that Daniel obeyed God instead of the king and his men, and Daniel was delivered from the mouths of lions. Have you considered, however, what led to Daniel's obedience and all the implications of how the story plays out? In this lesson, Dr. Thomas explains the opposition, obedience, deliverance, and triumph of Daniel.

LEARNING GOALS

When you have finished this lesson, you should be able to:

- Describe the opposition, obedience, deliverance, and triumph of Daniel
- Understand what led Daniel to be a man of obedience in Daniel 6
- Grasp the importance of cultivating godly habits

KEY IDEAS

- Daniel thrived in the midst of hostility.
- We are called to faithfully live out our vocation just as Daniel did.
- God is merciful and can change hearts of stone and turn the events of history in a single moment.

REFLECTION & DISCUSSION QUESTIONS

Before the Video

What Do You Think?

Take a moment to answer the following questions. They will prepare you for the lecture.

- How would you describe the story of Daniel and the lions' den?

- Is there ever a time to delay obedience and what we know to be right and true?

Scripture Reading

> *For he is the living God, enduring forever; his kingdom shall never be destroyed, and his dominion shall be to the end. He delivers and rescues; he works signs and wonders in heaven and on earth, he who has saved Daniel from the power of the lions.*
>
> —Daniel 6:26–27

- How does the truth about God in these verses give the Christian courage to walk in obedience?

During the Video

Answer the following questions while you watch the video. They will guide you through the lecture.

Daniel's Opposition and Obedience *0:00–14:35*

- What was the purpose of Augustine's *The City of God*?

- What's the context of Daniel chapter 6?

- What other Bible character does Dr. Thomas point out as an example of a man who had a pattern of prayer?

- Why couldn't King Darius pardon Daniel or undo his decree?

Daniel's Deliverance and Triumph *14:35–23:20*

- What was John Newton's simple prayer in the midst of the storm at sea?

- What was King Darius' response to Daniel's being found safe in the den of lions?

After the Video

Answer the following questions after you have finished the lecture. They will help you identify and summarize the major points.

- How did Daniel view his position in Babylon? What application does this have for us?

  If you are in a group, have the members discuss how they can be salt and light within their culture and vocations.

- Why is it important to regularly engage in the spiritual disciplines of Bible reading and prayer?

  If you are in a group, have the members discuss the benefits they have personally experienced as they've engaged in the spiritual disciplines.

- Describe a time when you were courageous.

  If you are in a group, have the members encourage one another to be courageous by sharing passages of Scripture that they use to combat fear.

PRAYER

Commit what you have learned from God's Word in this lesson to prayer.

- Praise God that His grace and mercy are abundant and that He melts hardened hearts of stone.
- Confess areas where you've given in to fear and compromise rather than exhibiting courage and obedience.
- Thank God for the faithful men and women in Scripture who were examples of obedience and prayer.
- Ask God to give you courage for whatever you are currently facing.

REVIEW QUIZ

Use these multiple-choice questions to measure what you learned from this lesson.

1. What age was Daniel when Jerusalem collapsed under the Babylonians, and what age was he when the events of Daniel 6 occurred?
   a. He was an infant at the fall of Jerusalem and a teenager during the events of Daniel 6.
   b. He was a small child at the fall of Jerusalem and a young adult during the events of Daniel 6.
   c. He was a teenager at the fall of Jerusalem and in his eighties during the events of Daniel 6.
   d. He was a young adult during both times because the events of Daniel 6 occurred right after the exile.

2. Why were Daniel's subordinates envious?
   a. Daniel was excelling beyond them.
   b. Daniel was holier than they.
   c. Daniel was older than they.
   d. Daniel was younger than they.

3. What was the first thing that Daniel did when he heard the decree?
   a. He went home, closed the windows, and prayed.
   b. He went home and prayed before open windows.
   c. He got angry with God and cried out in frustration.
   d. He engaged in deep soul-searching about the matter.

4. What caused Daniel to fall into the trap of his subordinates?
   a. His rebellion against the edict
   b. His friendship with the king
   c. His obedience
   d. His hesitancy

5. What was the reason that Daniel was safe in the den of lions?
   a. Daniel escaped from the den of lions.
   b. God sent an angel to close the lions' mouths.
   c. Darius released Daniel from the den of lions.
   d. Daniel's subordinates repented and got him out.

6. Who said, "Courage is resistance to fear, mastery of fear—not the absence of it"?
   a. Sinclair Ferguson
   b. W.G.T. Shedd
   c. John Newton
   d. Mark Twain

Answer Key—God's Courage to Daniel

REFLECTION & DISCUSSION QUESTIONS

Before the Video

What Do You Think?

These are personal questions. The answers should be based on your own knowledge and experience.

Scripture Reading

- How does the truth about God in these verses give the Christian courage to walk in obedience?

  Obeying God often requires us to go against the culture and against what other people think. Sometimes it is hard to obey. The truths proclaimed in Daniel 6 about the character of God should give the believer confident hope that God is worth obeying. He is a God who is living and enduring, He's in control, He's a Deliverer and a Rescuer, and He does marvelous and miraculous works. The God who saved Daniel from the lions is the same God we follow and submit to today.

During the Video

Daniel's Opposition and Obedience

- What was the purpose of Augustine's *The City of God*?

  Augustine wrote The City of God *while the Western empire of Rome was collapsing. The empire had become Christian under Constantine's rule, and Augustine was facing a major cultural shift with the collapse of the empire. His purpose in writing this book was to remind believers that we live our lives for the city above that will remain, not the city here that will fade away.*

- What's the context of Daniel chapter 6?

  Daniel faced a new culture and way of life throughout the exile. By this point in time, he probably spoke a new language and had been given a new name. He had been engaged in a cultural war although he had risen in the political hierarchy. He was being challenged by his envious subordinates. Throughout all this, he maintained his faith and was still a prophet of the Lord.

- What other Bible character does Dr. Thomas point out as an example of a man who had a pattern of prayer?

  Nehemiah was a man of prayer. He served the Persian prince a generation after Daniel. Throughout the book of Nehemiah, we find Nehemiah's lengthy prayers recorded. When there came a moment when the king asked him a question and he had only a moment to answer, Nehemiah instinctively did what he always did—he petitioned the Lord for help. This was second nature to him in a difficult moment because it was Nehemiah's habit to turn to God in prayer.

- Why couldn't King Darius pardon Daniel or undo his decree?

  According to the laws of the Medes and the Persians, once a decree had been established, it could not be broken. Even though Darius liked Daniel, his hands were tied. There was nothing that he could do to reverse the decree in order to save Daniel. He had no choice other than to declare Daniel guilty and sentence him to the lions' den.

Daniel's Deliverance and Triumph

- What was John Newton's simple prayer in the midst of the storm at sea?

  John Newton cried out to God with a simple plea, "Lord, have mercy." Newton was a man who had cared nothing for God and His mercy, but God extended amazing grace to him by using that storm to melt his heart of stone. As Newton later penned, "Sovereign grace has power alone to subdue a heart of stone. And the moment grace is felt, then the hardest heart will melt."

- What was King Darius' response to Daniel's being found safe in the den of lions?

  The triumph of this story is that not only did Daniel come out of the lions' den unscathed, but Darius established a decree that promoted Daniel's God. Darius declared that everyone in the Persian Empire should fear Daniel's God. Praise for God's deliverance issued forth from the mouth of Darius. We don't know whether Darius was truly a repentant man who converted to the God of Israel, but it's clear that God did a mighty work.

After the Video

- How did Daniel view his position in Babylon? What application does this have for us?

  Daniel saw his vocation as a prophet as something that went hand in hand with his political position; they weren't compartmentalized. The Reformers had a robust view of the doctrine of vocation, by which people see their Christian faith and calling going together with their earthly jobs and positions. Daniel is a marvelous example of one who lived vocationally with faithfulness. He viewed his positions together for the purpose of serving the culture that he was a part of. He used his vocation to better that culture and to be salt and light within that culture.

- Why is it important to regularly engage in the spiritual disciplines of Bible reading and prayer?

  When Daniel went to pray, it wasn't something new. He didn't decide to start praying because of the edict; prayer was already a regular part of his life and his worship. It was natural for him to be bold in prayer because he had already cultivated a heart of prayer. So it is with us. When people flounder in times of adversity or situations of compromise, it's often because they haven't prepared themselves for those moments. We don't become men and women of the Word and prayer when the difficult times come. We run to God and His Word in difficult times when we've already cultivated regular patterns of communing with God.

- Describe a time when you were courageous.

  This is a personal question; the answer should be based on your own experience. Answers might include a time of standing on one's convictions without compromise regardless of the consequences. Perhaps you've experienced God's giving you courage to share the gospel with a friend or family member when you were afraid to do so. Or maybe you had courage to step out in faith and pursue a new job, a new location, or a new ministry opportunity. God commands us to be courageous and not fear, and He gives us the grace and faith to do just that. He is with you in whatever He calls you to do.

REVIEW QUIZ

1. **C.**
   Daniel was only a teenager when Jerusalem was besieged by the Babylonians under Nebuchadnezzar's rule in 587 BC. Cyrus and Darius ruled in the 530s and 520s, so Daniel would have been in his eighties at the time of the events in Daniel 6.

2. **A.**
   Daniel's subordinates were envious because the things that Daniel did were marked by excellence, so they set up an ingenious trap by attacking Daniel's greatness, knowing how he would respond to the decree about praying to no one other than the king.

3. **B.**
   Daniel's immediate response was to go home and pray before open windows, just as he always had. He didn't stop and consider what to do. He immediately obeyed God rather than men without hesitation or seeking a way around the decree.

4. **C.**
   Daniel surely knew the trap that was set before him, and he had a choice: he could disobey and avoid the trap set before him, or he could obey and fall prey to what the men had anticipated and planned for him. Daniel was faithful and chose obedience.

5. **B.**
   The morning after Daniel had been thrown into the lions' den, Darius went to check on him. He had seen Daniel's faith and was possibly curious to know what had happened. He found Daniel without a scratch because God had sent an angel to keep the mouth of every lion closed.

6. **D.**
   Although Mark Twain was not a Christian, he was on to something regarding cour-

age. If there were nothing to fear, then there would be no need for courage. Courage is needed precisely because there are fearful things in this world. Yet as believers, we know the One who holds all things, and we can walk, by His grace, in courage.

7

God's Reassurance through John the Baptist

INTRODUCTION

What image comes to mind when you think of John the Baptist? Perhaps you envision a kind of wild man who lived in the wilderness, ate strange food, and wore uncomfortable clothes. You may immediately think that John was a man who proclaimed the coming Messiah and preached repentance to the people of Israel, but you may not have thought of him as a man who faltered in his faith. In this lesson, Dr. Thomas explains John the Baptist's courageous preaching, his loss of faith, and his death, using Mark 6 and Luke 7.

LEARNING GOALS

When you have finished this lesson, you should be able to:

- Describe John the Baptist, his ministry, and his message
- Discuss the nature of discipleship to Jesus Christ
- Explain what typically results from martyrdom

KEY IDEAS

- John the Baptist was not the Christ, but he had the important task of bearing witness to the coming Christ.
- John the Baptist faced imprisonment for faithfully preaching God's truth.
- Disciples are not superheroes; they are mere human beings.

REFLECTION & DISCUSSION QUESTIONS

Before the Video

What Do You Think?

Take a moment to answer the following questions. They will prepare you for the lecture.

- What is most remarkable about John the Baptist and his ministry?

- Why do disciples of Christ falter in their faith?

Scripture Reading

As it is written in Isaiah the prophet, "Behold, I send my messenger before your face, who will prepare your way, the voice of one crying in the wilderness: 'Prepare the way of the Lord, make his paths straight,'" John appeared, baptizing in the wilderness and proclaiming a baptism of repentance for the forgiveness of sins.

—Mark 1:2–4

- In what way does this passage set apart John's ministry as unique?

During the Video

Answer the following questions while you watch the video. They will guide you through the lecture.

John the Baptist *0:00–12:10*

- What was the significance of Jesus' saying that the one who is least in the kingdom of God is greater than John the Baptist?

- Jesus' second statement about John the Baptist was that "among those born of women none is greater than John" (Luke 7:28). What was the significance of that statement?

John's Doubt and Death *12:10–23:33*

- According to Dr. Thomas' conjectures, why might John the Baptist have begun to doubt whether Jesus was really the awaited Messiah?

- What does Dr. Thomas say "gives us a measure of assurance in our failing and faltering discipleship"?
- What eventually happened to Herod and Herodias after the death of John the Baptist?

After the Video

Answer the following questions after you have finished the lecture. They will help you identify and summarize the major points.

- What was the effect of John the Baptist's preaching on Herod Antipas? What does this suggest about John's ministry and God's Word?

  If you are in a group, have the members discuss the power of the gospel faithfully preached. Have them describe instances when they have seen someone convicted by the truth of God's Word, even if the person had been unwilling to bow in submission to it.
- Can a true disciple of Christ ever question God's providence? Why or why not?

  If you are in a group, have the members discuss times when they have wrestled with God's providence and the place in which they found themselves.
- Toward the end of the lesson, Dr. Thomas leaves us with an important question for consideration: What would you be willing to die for?

  If you are in a group, have the members spend time praying that God would grant them the grace and courage to live for Him and even to die for Him if He should so choose.

PRAYER

Commit what you have learned from God's Word in this lesson to prayer.

- Praise God for fulfilled prophecy that assures us of the faithfulness of His Word.
- Confess times when you have lacked courage in sharing the gospel of Jesus Christ with others.
- Thank God for recording testimonies of human limitations and weakness in Scripture, that we might be encouraged in our faith.
- Ask God to preserve and grow your faith as you seek to follow Him as a faithful disciple.

REVIEW QUIZ

Use these multiple-choice questions to measure what you learned from this lesson.

1. What did Thomas Cranmer do as an act of repentance for the lapse of faith that he had expressed?
   a. He asked to be burned at the stake.
   b. He thrust his right hand into the flame.
   c. As the flames rose, he cried out in repentance.
   d. He wrote a recantation of his former recantation of faith.
2. John the Baptist accused Herod Antipas of breaking Levitical law by doing what?
   a. Marrying his niece
   b. Marrying his sister
   c. Marrying multiple women
   d. Marrying his brother's ex-wife
3. Where was John the Baptist imprisoned?
   a. Masada
   b. Jerusalem
   c. Herodium
   d. Machaerus
4. John the Baptist's message did not emphasize forgiveness.
   a. True
   b. False
5. Herodias died a peaceful death despite her treachery against John the Baptist.
   a. True
   b. False
6. According to Tertullian, what was the second-century church built on?
   a. The prayers of the saints
   b. The blood of the martyrs
   c. The canonization of Scripture
   d. The preaching of John the Baptist

Answer Key—God's Reassurance through John the Baptist

REFLECTION & DISCUSSION QUESTIONS

Before the Video

What Do You Think?

These are personal questions. The answers should be based on your own knowledge and experience.

Scripture Reading

- In what way does this passage set apart John's ministry as unique?

  Isaiah had prophesied that one would come before the Messiah, announcing His coming and preparing the way for Him (see Isa. 40). John the Baptist was not just another preacher. John the Baptist's ministry was a fulfillment of prophecy. Not only did his message bear truth and weight, but the fact that this prophecy was fulfilled by John the Baptist adds validity to his message as well as to the truth that Jesus is the Messiah.

During the Video

John the Baptist

- What was the significance of Jesus' saying that the one who is least in the kingdom of God is greater than John the Baptist?

  Jesus was referring to the old and new covenants in this statement. John the Baptist had been right at the end of the old covenant. He was making the way and pointing toward Jesus Christ, who was coming to fulfill all the promises of the old covenant. Jesus' statement indicated that a new covenant was beginning, one in which the promises of the old covenant would be fulfilled.

- Jesus' second statement about John the Baptist was that "among those born of women none is greater than John" (Luke 7:28). What was the significance of that statement?

  This statement seems to be the opposite of the first one because it focuses on John the Baptist's greatness. John was a great prophet—according to Jesus, he was the greatest of all the prophets. When Elizabeth was pregnant with John, the angel told Zechariah that John would be great, would be filled with the Holy Spirit, and would turn many to the Lord. His job as a prophet was to announce the coming Messiah, preaching the message of judgment for those who would not repent and of grace for all who would turn to Jesus as the Messiah.

John's Doubt and Death

- According to Dr. Thomas' conjectures, why might John the Baptist have begun to doubt whether Jesus was really the awaited Messiah?

  It's hard to say exactly, but John might have been suffering under the effects of imprisonment. That could be wearying for anyone, even John the Baptist. In addition, John had preached a warning of judgment and the urgency to repent and believe in the Messiah. Perhaps John felt confused, unsure how to understand that the kingdom of God had come, yet Herod was still in power and he was the one in prison. This was probably perplexing and disheartening.

- What does Dr. Thomas say "gives us a measure of assurance in our failing and faltering discipleship"?

  According to Dr. Thomas, the Scripture's inclusion of men like John the Baptist's and Elijah's stumbling gives us encouragement. We all stumble at various times, in various ways. If John the Baptist and Elijah stumbled, we can take heart. These were men who walked by faith and saw great miracles, yet their faith faltered and they displayed human weakness at times. Stumbling in our faith and having moments of doubt and discouragement does not mean that we can never be restored again.

- What eventually happened to Herod and Herodias after the death of John the Baptist?

  There was a falling-out with Emperor Caligula, and they were banished from Judea. They went to northern Spain, which was the most remote part of the kingdom at that time. It is understood that Herodias was walking on a frozen lake and she died by drowning when the ice gave way. It seems that she faced an awful death herself.

After the Video

- What was the effect of John the Baptist's preaching on Herod Antipas? What does this suggest about John's ministry and God's Word?

  Interestingly enough, Herod Antipas feared John the Baptist, according to Mark 6:20. Herod saw that John was "a righteous and holy man," and because of this "he kept him safe." It appears that John was faithful to preach the message of the kingdom to Herod from prison because the verse continues with the statement that Herod "heard him, he was greatly perplexed, and yet he heard him gladly." John the Baptist was faithful to proclaim the truth of God, and he must have built rapport with Herod so that Herod would go to John in prison and gladly hear what he had to say. This seems to give testimony to both the power of God's Word and the power of John's witness.

- Can a true disciple of Christ ever question God's providence? Why or why not?

  While heroes are typically thought of as those without weakness and those who never waver, that is not an accurate view of discipleship. God created us as humans with limitations, and we must depend on the Lord. There are several examples in the Bible, Jesus included, of those who pleaded with God for something different. Paul asked God to remove his thorn in the flesh. Jesus asked the Father to remove the cup from Him in the garden of Gethsemane. Another great example is that of Habakkuk. He wrestled with God in prayer after God answered his prayer differently than he expected. In all these examples, though, the attitude is that of humility, along with a willingness to ultimately submit to God and His ways.

- Toward the end of the lesson, Dr. Thomas leaves us with an important question for consideration: What would you be willing to die for?

  This is a personal question that requires individual reflection. As you consider what you would be willing to die for, the question is quite sobering. Many people might think of their spouse, their children, and other family members. Perhaps some would be willing to die for a close friend. We may think of people who are willing to die for noble causes and to protect their country. But what about your faith? Would you be willing to face martyrdom for Christ and the gospel? As you personally reflect on this question, meditate on Philippians 1:21: "For to me to live is Christ, and to die is gain." Our lives should be spent for Christ, and dying should be gain because we will be ushered into His presence.

REVIEW QUIZ

1. **B.**

   Thomas Cranmer, the archbishop under Henry VIII and Edward VI, lived during the reign of "Bloody Mary." When he was accused of heresy, he wrote a sermon recanting his evangelical faith. Instead of delivering the sermon that he had written, however, he preached the truth of the gospel and said that the hand that had written that recantation would be the first to go into the flames at his time of death.

2. **A.**

   Herod Antipas had married Herodias, who was his brother Philip's ex-wife. The issue here, however, was that Herodias was the daughter of Herod's half-brother, making her his niece. This was forbidden under Levitical law, according to the laws of consanguinity in the book of Leviticus.

3. **D.**

   Machaerus was the summer palace of Herod Antipas. It was located high up in the hills on a rocky promontory on the northeast side of the Dead Sea. The luxurious palace had been built by Herod Antipas' grandfather, Herod the Great.

4. **B.**
John's mission for his entire life was to point to Christ. His message was, "Behold, the Lamb of God, who takes away the sin of the world!" (John 1:29). While John did preach repentance, it was always in light of the coming Messiah.

5. **B.**
Herodias' daughter, Salome, danced before Herod and his guests, and he offered her anything, up to half his kingdom. When Salome queried her mother about what to ask for, Herodias told her to ask for the head of John the Baptist on a platter because she had a grudge against him. Herodias herself would die a sudden death, much in the same way that John the Baptist had died. It is attested that she fell into a frozen lake.

6. **B.**
According to Tertullian, the church was built on the blood of the martyrs. That might seem like quite a bold statement, but consider what dying for Christ communicates to the onlooking world: it validates the truth of the message. People die only for what they truly value, love, and believe in. The martyrdom of the disciples led to the spread of the gospel and the growth of the church.

8

God's Boldness to Peter & John

INTRODUCTION

How would you respond if you were told that you could no longer talk about Jesus? Currently in America, there is still much freedom, yet even today, there are increasing government restrictions on some matters that relate to truths of Scripture. The Apostles, however, faced open opposition and the restraint of their ministry, as do many Christians throughout the world today. In this lesson, Dr. Thomas looks at how Peter and John boldly proclaimed Christ and the gospel amid great opposition by the Sanhedrin.

LEARNING GOALS

When you have finished this lesson, you should be able to:

- Describe the circumstances leading to Peter and John's imprisonment
- Explain the transformation of Peter from fearful to courageous
- Discuss obedience to God and obedience to the governing authorities

KEY IDEAS

- Peter and John preached the message of Christ with boldness and courage under the conviction that it is better to obey God than to obey man.
- There is salvation in no one else but Jesus Christ.
- Believers ought to exude Christian character because of the transformation that Christ has worked in their lives.

REFLECTION & DISCUSSION QUESTIONS

Before the Video

What Do You Think?

Take a moment to answer the following questions. They will prepare you for the lecture.

- What is central to the gospel message?

- What do you think caused the transformation in Peter from a man who denied Christ to the bold Apostle on whom Christ would build His church?

Scripture Reading

There is no fear in love, but perfect love casts out fear. For fear has to do with punishment, and whoever fears has not been perfected in love.

—1 John 4:18

- As you prepare for this lesson, consider the power of fear and the power of love. How does perfect love cast out fear?

During the Video

Answer the following questions while you watch the video. They will guide you through the lecture.

Context *0:00–9:03*

- What does *Anastasia* mean? Why is it critical to the gospel?

- Peter had denied Christ three times during His arrest and trial. In the events recorded in Acts 4, Peter was bold and courageous. What had happened to Peter?

Peter's Message *9:03–24:02*

- What was the personal significance for Peter in quoting from Psalm 118 during his sermon?

- What did the Sanhedrin order Peter and John to do, and what was their response?

After the Video

Answer the following questions after you have finished the lecture. They will help you identify and summarize the major points.

- According to Dr. Thomas, what is the application of Ephesians 5:18 when it tells us to "be filled with the Spirit"?

  This verse can be easily misunderstood and can even create controversy. If you are in a group, have the members discuss what their understanding of this verse has been. Ask: How do you think this verse applies to believers today?

- How do we determine whether or not to disobey governing authorities?

  If you are in a group, have the members read Romans 13:1–7. Ask: What principles can be gleaned from this passage to help us understand our relationship to authority, whether it be to the government or to an employer, for example?

- What was the one quality that stood out about Peter, John, and the other eyewitnesses of Jesus? Why do you think this was the case?

  If you are in a group, have the members discuss how they can grow in exuding Christlike character in their lives and how they can overflow with the gospel in their speech.

PRAYER

Commit what you have learned from God's Word in this lesson to prayer.

- Praise God for sending the Holy Spirit to be our Advocate and Helper.
- Confess ways that you have lacked boldness and courage for your Christian convictions.
- Thank God for supplying us with boldness and courage that we do not have in and of ourselves.
- Ask God to fill you with the Spirit so that you would be empowered to deal with whatever tasks, trials, or decisions you face.

REVIEW QUIZ

Use these multiple-choice questions to measure what you learned from this lesson.

1. What "notable sign" did the Sanhedrin refer to?
   a. The many signs and wonders being performed by the Apostles
   b. The healing of the crippled man at Solomon's Portico
   c. The salvation of Paul on the road to Damascus
   d. The bodily resurrection of Jesus Christ

2. Who were the Sanhedrin?
   a. Seventy-one elders and rabbis
   b. The leaders of the early Christian church
   c. The rabbis specifically trained by Gamaliel
   d. Pharisees charged with keeping Christianity in check

3. *Paraklētos* means "advocate" or "helper."
   a. True
   b. False

4. What was *not* central to Peter's message?
   a. Jesus as the Advocate and Helper
   b. Jesus as the Savior of sinners
   c. Jesus as raised from the dead
   d. Jesus as Lord and Messiah

5. What kind of message does Peter preach?
   a. A message of generous orthodoxy
   b. A message free of judgment
   c. A message of exclusivity
   d. A message of inclusivity

6. What astonished the Sanhedrin about Peter and John?
   a. They were surprised by Peter's boldness.
   b. They were surprised by the content of Peter's message.
   c. They were surprised that Peter and John were not educated.
   d. They were surprised that Peter and John refused to obey their order.

Answer Key—God's Boldness to Peter & John

REFLECTION & DISCUSSION QUESTIONS

Before the Video

What Do You Think?

These are personal questions. The answers should be based on your own knowledge and experience.

Scripture Reading

- As you prepare for this lesson, consider the power of fear and the power of love. How does perfect love cast out fear?

  We've all experienced the crippling effects of fear in big and small ways. Fear is powerful. But according to this verse, we know that there is something more powerful than fear: love. In the verses leading up to this one, we read that God is love and that He loved us enough to send His Son to be the propitiation for our sins. Love, particularly covenant love, brings rest and security. When we rest in God's love for us—in the truths of the gospel and of a God who has covenanted Himself to us—God becomes bigger to us than other people and things that may be fearful. We are able to rightly view what is fearful in light of who God is and His love for us. This produces rest, security, boldness, and courage.

During the Video

Context

- What does *Anastasia* mean? Why is it critical to the gospel?

  Anastasia *means "resurrection." The bodily resurrection of Christ was the central message of early Christianity. Through the resurrection of Christ, the veracity and truthfulness of everything Christ had taught and preached was confirmed. In 1 Corinthians 15:1–5, the Apostle Paul includes the resurrection in the gospel that he proclaimed because without the resurrection, we do not have a complete gospel message.*

- Peter had denied Christ three times during His arrest and trial. In the events recorded in Acts 4, Peter was bold and courageous. What had happened to Peter?

  According to Dr. Thomas, Pentecost is what had happened to Peter. Acts 4:8 introduces Peter's response to the Sanhedrin with this: "Then Peter, filled with the Holy

Spirit, said to them . . ." Peter was bold and courageous because he was filled with the Holy Spirit, and he no longer walked in fear and denial.

Peter's Message

- What was the personal significance for Peter in quoting from Psalm 118 during his sermon?

  In Psalm 118, Peter referenced the cornerstone that had been rejected, and this was significant for Peter because his name was petros *or* petra. *Dr. Thomas points out that Peter probably had a fascination with rocks and stones from the day that Jesus drew out the significance of his name (see Matt. 16:13–18). Peter made numerous references to rocks and stones throughout 1 Peter.*

- What did the Sanhedrin order Peter and John to do, and what was their response?

  The Sanhedrin had no response to Peter's bold message; neither could they ignore or dismiss the healing of the crippled man. The Sanhedrin commanded Peter and John to no longer "speak or teach at all in the name of Jesus" (Acts 4:18). Peter and John could not obey such a command. They said that it was better to obey God than man, and they replied, "We cannot but speak of what we have seen and heard" (v. 20).

After the Video

- According to Dr. Thomas, what is the application of Ephesians 5:18 when it tells us to "be filled with the Spirit"?

  The filling and refilling of the Spirit should be an ongoing experience in the believer's life because Ephesians 5:18 is an exhortation given to the church. Dr. Thomas notes that the filling of the Spirit is especially important when entering an act of ministry, trials, difficulties, and decisions. He says that believers ought to pray for the filling of our Helper and Advocate in order that we might overflow with the Spirit, who was sent to us by Christ to minister to us.

- How do we determine whether or not to disobey governing authorities?

  Scripture is clear that we are to obey the government and our governing authorities. Jesus and the Apostles addressed this matter (see Matt. 22:15–22; Rom. 13). The point at which obedience stops, however, is when the governing authorities demand direct disobedience to God. If asked to do something against God's will and directly against Scripture, our response ought to be similar to Peter's and John's: we ought to continue preaching Christ and obeying God with great courage.

- What was the one quality that stood out about Peter, John, and the other eyewitnesses of Jesus? Why do you think this was the case?

  The Sanhedrin saw uneducated, common men who they believed had no business interpreting the Scriptures. What could not be denied was the fact that these men and the other men and women who had walked with Jesus could not stop talking about Him. Peter and John said that they couldn't help themselves; Jesus just overflowed from them. They had been transformed by their Savior, and they had witnessed others be transformed by Him as well. It was too much to contain, and they had to speak of all they had seen, heard, and experienced.

REVIEW QUIZ

1. **B.**
   In Acts 3, Peter and John had healed a crippled man at Solomon's Portico. The man had been crippled since his youth and was in his forties when he was healed. He asked Peter and John for money, but they instead healed him in Christ's name. Everyone knew what had happened, and the Sanhedrin couldn't hide it or stop people from talking about it.

2. **A.**
   The Sanhedrin were seventy-one elders and rabbis of Israel. They would have been similar to a supreme court. They heard and ruled on matters that came to them from lesser courts. The Sanhedrin did not approve of the Christian church and were facing the rapid growth of the church after Christ's resurrection and Pentecost.

3. **A.**
   The paraklētos *is the Holy Spirit. He was the Advocate and Helper promised by Jesus Christ in John 14–17. This promise was fulfilled at Pentecost when the Holy Spirit came and filled the church with power.*

4. **A.**
   Jesus was the central message of Peter's sermon before the Sanhedrin in Acts 4:8–12. He preached Christ as Savior, Lord, and Messiah. Peter accused them of crucifying Christ and attributed the raising of Jesus from the dead to God the Father. He did not, however, emphasize Jesus as a paraklētos, *though we do well to look to Him as such.*

5. **C.**
   Peter concluded his message by saying that salvation is through no one else but Christ and that it is only by His name that we can be saved. This is an exclusive message. The cry for universalism or inclusivism goes directly against the teachings of the entire New Testament, including the teaching of Jesus Himself. This was and is a bold, difficult, and countercultural message, but it is the one that people need to hear.

6. **C.**
   After Peter finished preaching, the Sanhedrin noted his boldness, but what was most astonishing was that he and John were "uneducated, common men" (Acts 4:13). The Greek words used here indicate that the Sanhedrin thought of them as

unschooled idiots who didn't understand basic grammar. Given the sermon that Peter preached, it should be astonishing to us that he and John were not trained students of the Scriptures.

9

God's Salvation through Paul & Silas at Philippi

INTRODUCTION

In Acts 16, we find Paul and Silas proclaiming the gospel in Philippi. We meet three individuals throughout this account, and we see the dramatic, marvelous work of God's grace up close. As Paul and Silas faithfully minister the gospel, they find themselves imprisoned as a result. In this lesson, Dr. Thomas focuses our attention on the unique stories of conversion and the way of salvation.

LEARNING GOALS

When you have finished this lesson, you should be able to:

- Describe the three conversion stories in the Acts 16 narrative
- Discuss the significance of the jailer's question to Paul and Silas
- Grasp the beauty of God's varied ways in saving sinners

KEY IDEAS

- No matter a person's current circumstances, the grace of God remains unmatched in power and effectiveness.
- While conversion stories may look different, there is only one way to be saved.
- Praying and singing are powerful weapons in the face of hardship.

REFLECTION & DISCUSSION QUESTIONS

Before the Video

What Do You Think?

Take a moment to answer the following questions. They will prepare you for the lecture.

- Think of dramatic conversion stories and testimonies that you have heard. How did those stories encourage your faith?

- What is the most important question that each person must wrestle with?

Scripture Reading

But God, being rich in mercy, because of the great love with which he loved us, even when we were dead in our trespasses, made us alive together with Christ—by grace you have been saved. . . . For by grace you have been saved through faith. And this is not your own doing; it is the gift of God, not a result of works, so that no one may boast.

—Ephesians 2:4–5, 8–9

- How is the importance of God's grace underscored in this passage?

During the Video

Answer the following questions while you watch the video. They will guide you through the lecture.

Three Unlikely Converts *0:00–10:29*

- What part does Luke play in this narrative?

- The slave girl with the evil spirit first spoke truth about Paul and the Apostles. Why did an evil spirit declare a true statement?

- Describe what happened as Paul and Silas were put in prison and their response.

The Way of Salvation *10:29–22:57*

- What is the most important question that a person can ask?

- What is the *oikos* formula?

- Summarize the three conversion stories from Acts 16.

After the Video

Answer the following questions after you have finished the lecture. They will help you identify and summarize the major points.

- Reflect on the following lines from William Cowper's poem: "His purposes will ripen fast, unfolding every hour. The bud may have a bitter taste, but sweet will be the flower." What does this mean?

  If you are in a group, have the members share a time when God encouraged them and brought them through a bitter experience that He worked for their good.

- Explain why the answer found in Scripture for how to be saved is sometimes "believe" and other times "repent and believe." Give an example from Scripture.

  If you are in a group, have the members discuss how understanding this might help them address people they are evangelizing.

- Is it necessary for a person's conversion to be dramatic? Why or why not?

  If you are in a group, have the members take a few moments to briefly share their own conversion stories, rejoicing in God's gift of grace.

PRAYER

Commit what you have learned from God's Word in this lesson to prayer.

- Praise God for His infinite, marvelous, and matchless grace.
- Confess ways that you have minimized grace and sought to perform in order to earn righteousness.
- Thank God for the conversion story that He wrote on the pages of your life.
- Ask God to save the lost among your family, friends, and community.

REVIEW QUIZ

Use these multiple-choice questions to measure what you learned from this lesson.

1. Who is *not* converted in Acts 16?
   a. A slave girl
   b. A jailer
   c. A leper
   d. Lydia

2. Which statement best summarizes the reason why Paul and Silas were arrested?
   a. Paul and Silas were preaching in the agora, which was forbidden.
   b. Lydia and her household were baptized after the Lord opened her heart.
   c. Paul and Silas were going to a place to pray, most likely near the river, which was sacred.
   d. Paul commanded the evil spirit to leave the girl, and this produced a loss of income for her owners.

3. The Philippian jailer was called to repent after asking about what he needed to do to be saved.
   a. True
   b. False

4. Although all the stories in this narrative are different, what is the one commonality?
   a. The households of all three people were also baptized.
   b. All three people were immediately baptized.
   c. All three people were saved out of similar backgrounds and situations.
   d. All three people received the gift of salvation; they were all saved by grace.

5. Which of the following did God use in Dr. Thomas' own conversion?
   a. The gospel of Luke
   b. John Stott's *Basic Christianity*
   c. Jonathan Edwards' "Sinners in the Hands of an Angry God"
   d. Jonathan Edwards' *A Narrative of Surprising Conversions*

6. What best summarizes the concluding application of this narrative?
   a. Salvation is possible if we are obedient before we believe.
   b. Christians, if imprisoned, will be released through quick and miraculous means.
   c. Salvation is possible in the name of the Lord Jesus Christ and in His name alone.
   d. Christians should follow the model of the Apostles and seek after dramatic conversions.

Answer Key—God's Salvation through Paul & Silas at Philippi

REFLECTION & DISCUSSION QUESTIONS

Before the Video

What Do You Think?

These are personal questions. The answers should be based on your own knowledge and experience.

Scripture Reading

- How is the importance of God's grace underscored in this passage?

  Ephesians 2 is a beautiful passage of Scripture in which the gospel is clearly explained. We are all, by our very natures, lost. We were dead in our sins, unable to atone for them and make right our standing with God. But this passage underscores the importance of God's grace. The phrase "by grace you have been saved" appears twice. These instances are preceded by the reality of our being dead in trespasses, so our being made alive in Christ can be only the result of God's grace and not our works.

During the Video

Three Unlikely Converts

- What part does Luke play in this narrative?

  Luke is the author of the book of Acts. Yet he was not only an author or a historian; he was an eyewitness of these events. We know this because in Acts 16:16, Luke uses the personal pronoun "we" twice, indicating that he was with Paul and Silas. He was an eyewitness to these miraculous conversions that were brought about by the Holy Spirit.

- The slave girl with the evil spirit first spoke truth about Paul and the Apostles. Why did an evil spirit declare a true statement?

  The statement that the girl made was this: "These men are servants of the Most High God, who proclaim to you the way of salvation" (Acts 16:17). This statement was true, and that was precisely the scheme of the evil spirit. If the evil spirit came right out with a bald-faced lie, it wouldn't have been as convincing. On the other hand, if the evil spirit told numerous truths and then a lie, a person would be much more susceptible to believing the lie. This is the deceptive, crafty nature of the evil one.

- Describe what happened as Paul and Silas were put in prison and their response.

  The official attendants of the district were called lictors, *which literally means "rod beaters." Their name alone indicates what Paul and Silas went through. They were stripped of their garments, beaten with rods, and put into the inner prison, where their feet were fastened in stocks. Paul and Silas didn't respond in self-pity or in cries to God to release them. They cried out to God in prayer and in the singing of hymns.*

The Way of Salvation

- What is the most important question that a person can ask?

  Of all the questions that we do and can ask, the most important is this: "What must I do to be saved?" This is the most important question because we are, by nature, lost. Apart from Christ, we have no hope; therefore, we need to be saved by the Savior, Jesus Christ. Our souls hang in the balance between heaven and hell based on this question and where we turn for the answer.

- What is the *oikos* formula?

  Oikos *means "household." After the jailer cared for Paul and Silas, he and his household were baptized. So the* oikos *formula refers to the household baptisms in Acts. Dr. Thomas views the* oikos *formula as the doctrine of covenant, that salvation is promised not just to the individual but to the person's children also. Dr. Steven Lawson, however, would say that the jailer's children were adults and would have made their own professions of faith. Regardless, God did a great work of grace in this family.*

- Summarize the three conversion stories from Acts 16.

  The first convert, Lydia, was saved through the careful exposition of Scripture. Then, as Paul and Silas went to a place of prayer, they were followed by a slave girl possessed by an evil spirit. She was converted by a powerful exorcism. Finally, the Philippian jailer was converted through listening to Paul and Silas' prayers and singing, witnessing an earthquake, and realizing his own need for salvation.

After the Video

- Reflect on the following lines from William Cowper's poem: "His purposes will ripen fast, unfolding every hour. The bud may have a bitter taste, but sweet will be the flower." What does this mean?

  Cowper's poem speaks of God's mysterious providence that we do not always see or understand from the outset. Just as a bud may at first be bitter and need time to ripen, so our circumstances may taste bitter. Sometimes it is difficult to see through the darkness and realize that there might be anything else on the other side of our present circumstances, but this poem reminds us that ripening is occurring, which means that sweetness is coming. Paul had a firm belief in the providence of God. Later, when Paul was writing to the Philippian church from prison in Rome, he told them that God was in control and was using his imprisonment to advance the gospel. Paul was able to see beyond his circumstances to the higher providence and goodness of God. May we grow in our understanding and ability to see our circumstances from this perspective of trust.

- Explain why the answer found in Scripture for how to be saved is sometimes "believe" and other times "repent and believe." Give an example from Scripture.

  In the account of the Philippian jailer, Paul answered his question with "Believe in the Lord Jesus, and you will be saved" (Acts 16:31). The jailer already had a very acute awareness of his sin and neediness and therefore did not need to be told to repent. On the other hand, if someone is not yet aware of his or her sin and state of need, the person needs to be made aware. When Jesus answered the rich young ruler, who had the same question, Jesus pointed him to the Ten Commandments. This was not because the man needed to follow them to earn his righteousness. Rather, he needed to see that he could not keep the law and to understand that he was a sinner who needed to repent. Without knowledge of sin and understanding the need to be saved, a person has no reason to believe in the Lord Jesus Christ.

- Is it necessary for a person's conversion to be dramatic? Why or why not?

  In discussing the different stories found within this narrative, Dr. Thomas points out how different all our stories are. In this narrative, the people have dramatic conversions. Dr. Thomas mentions Jeremiah and John the Baptist, who were apparently converted in the womb, as counterexamples to these dramatic conversions. As César Malan stated, "Some people are drawn to Christ like a mother puts a child to sleep with a kiss." Some conversions are gentle and quiet without any flashy lights or dramatic effects. That doesn't change the validity of one's conversion because conversion is about the grace of God as it reaches into a person's dead heart, giving the person life and faith. Ephesians 2 is every person's story of conversion regardless of the circumstances surrounding it.

REVIEW QUIZ

1. **C.**
   Borrowing from Jonathan Edwards, Dr. Thomas describes Acts 16 as "a narrative of surprising conversions." This account includes the conversions of Lydia, a fortune-telling slave girl, and the Philippian jailer. It is an amazing narrative in which God's power and grace are evident in these individuals' unique stories.

2. **D.**
   Paul and Silas were imprisoned after Paul commanded the evil spirit to leave the girl. The slave owners were not happy about this because it resulted in a direct loss of income for them. They seized Paul and Silas and took them before the rulers at the marketplace, accusing them of disturbing the city and going against Roman customs.

3. **B.**

   After the earthquake, the jailer awoke and saw the open prison doors. Assuming that all the prisoners had escaped, he braced himself to fall on his sword, since this had happened on his watch, but Paul stopped him, assuring him that the prisoners were all accounted for. The jailer cried out, "Sirs, what must I do to be saved?" He was a desperate man who understood his lost condition and need, and Paul called him simply to believe in the Lord Jesus Christ.

4. **D.**

   All these characters come from very different situations, but these accounts of salvation are all stories of God's grace and His amazing gift of salvation that is bestowed on undeserving sinners. The stories are different, and even the level of drama surrounding the conversions is different, but God's glorious grace is the same.

5. **B.**

   Before his salvation, Dr. Thomas was an agnostic. He was given a copy of John Stott's Basic Christianity *in college by his best friend from high school. After putting it off for several months, Dr. Thomas finally read it, and he came to faith in Jesus Christ.*

6. **C.**

   This narrative serves as a warning and a blessed comfort to us. It is a warning to those who do not know Christ to come to their senses and forsake the way of foolishness and death. For those who know Christ Jesus as their Savior, it is a reminder of sweet comfort that they, too, have been saved by the power of the Holy Spirit.

10

God's Assurance & Paul's Final Imprisonment

INTRODUCTION

Throughout Paul's life and ministry, he faced much hardship and persecution. In the midst of his sufferings, we have some of the richest letters written to the church and to individuals within the church. Second Timothy is one such letter. Through this letter, we gain a heartfelt and personal glimpse into Paul. In this lesson, Dr. Thomas sets the stage and explains key elements of Paul's final imprisonment and the things for which he longed during his last days.

LEARNING GOALS

When you have finished this lesson, you should be able to:

- Describe the context of Paul's imprisonment
- Understand the importance of relationships and companionship
- Describe what Paul missed during his imprisonment and why

KEY IDEAS

- Paul was imprisoned more than once, and during his final imprisonment he wrote 2 Timothy.
- While in prison, Paul longed for both practical and spiritual things.
- Even during his last days, Paul remained faithful, his mind being set on the gospel of the Lord Jesus Christ.

REFLECTION & DISCUSSION QUESTIONS

Before the Video

What Do You Think?

Take a moment to answer the following questions. They will prepare you for the lecture.

- How would you describe Paul's ministry?

- What do you know about Paul's imprisonments?

Scripture Reading

I have fought the good fight, I have finished the race, I have kept the faith. Henceforth there is laid up for me the crown of righteousness, which the Lord, the righteous judge, will award to me on that day, and not only to me but also to all who have loved his appearing.

—2 Timothy 4:7–8

- What does it mean for the believer to fight the good fight, finish the race, and keep the faith as Paul describes in these verses?

During the Video

Answer the following questions while you watch the video. They will guide you through the lecture.

Paul's Imprisonment and Loss of Company *0:00–14:21*

- What was the reign of Nero characterized by?

- When and how did Paul die?

- Who were the four people that Paul particularly missed?

Paul's Practical and Spiritual Longings *14:21–23:35*

- In the 1500s, who wrote a letter with a request like Paul's, and why?

- What was significant about Paul's wanting "the parchments" (2 Tim. 4:13)?

- When everyone else deserted Paul at his trial, who stood by him?

After the Video

Answer the following questions after you have finished the lecture. They will help you identify and summarize the major points.

- What did the Apostle Paul do, knowing that his death was imminent? What does this teach us?

  If you are in a group, have the members discuss what they would want their last words to be and to whom they would say them.

- What was so meaningful about Paul's request that Timothy come to him along with John Mark, and what is the lesson in this for us?

  If you are in a group, have the members discuss any ways that they have tried to make up with family members or friends and what they have seen God do through those attempts.

- What can we learn from both Paul's asking Timothy to bring him his cloak and Timothy's willingness to answer this request?

  If you are in a group, have the members share times when they either received or gave service in a similar way. What was the result of that service?

PRAYER

Commit what you have learned from God's Word in this lesson to prayer.

- Praise God for the ability to know and study His Word.
- Confess any ways that you have given in to the mindset that our end days here on this earth are for selfish gain rather than continued kingdom work.
- Thank God for any broken fellowship that has been restored and relationships that have been mended.
- Ask God that He would preserve and strengthen you to fight the good fight, finish the race, and keep the faith.

REVIEW QUIZ

Use these multiple-choice questions to measure what you learned from this lesson.

1. How many known episodes of imprisonments did Paul have, and what was the cumulative length?
   a. Two episodes totaling approximately six years
   b. Three episodes totaling approximately five and a half years
   c. Four episodes totaling approximately three years
   d. Five episodes totaling approximately five and a half years

2. Who risked his own potential arrest and execution to visit Paul in prison?
   a. Timothy
   b. Tychicus
   c. John Mark
   d. Onesiphorus

3. Who was Paul's protégé in the faith?
   a. Timothy
   b. Tychicus
   c. John Mark
   d. Onesiphorus

4. Who was present with Paul while he was imprisoned in Rome?
   a. Luke
   b. Linus
   c. Pudens
   d. Eubulus

5. Most likely, what were the parchments that Paul asked Timothy to bring?
   a. Writings from his own letters
   b. Writings of the philosophers
   c. Writings from the Hebrew Old Testament
   d. Writings from the Greek New Testament

6. In this passage, Paul made four longings known to Timothy of things he missed. Which of the following was *not* included?
   a. Clothes
   b. Freedom
   c. Company
   d. God's presence

Answer Key—God's Assurance & Paul's Final Imprisonment

REFLECTION & DISCUSSION QUESTIONS

Before the Video

What Do You Think?

These are personal questions. The answers should be based on your own knowledge and experience.

Scripture Reading

- What does it mean for the believer to fight the good fight, finish the race, and keep the faith as Paul describes in these verses?

  These words that Paul penned, knowing that the end was near, are beautiful. They are a testimony of God's grace, the preserving power of Christ, and the sanctifying work of the Holy Spirit. Paul's description is not that of physical prowess or stamina, but of spiritual endurance. He likens the Christian life to fighting and to a physical competition. As believers, we ought to press on in serving the Lord in this life so that we may get to the end, look back, and have that feeling of a good fight or race won. The goal is not perfection, but consistency and endurance. It is only by God's enabling grace and strength that we are able to keep the faith and persevere.

During the Video

Paul's Imprisonment and Loss of Company

- What was the reign of Nero characterized by?

  Nero is remembered for his savagery. He was accused of having the city set on fire in order that he might gain more land to erect buildings in his honor. He blamed the Christians for the fire and set about to distract and entertain the people through games. These games included persecution of Christians in which they fought wild animals and were used as torches to light these events. This was a truly grotesque and intense time.

- When and how did Paul die?

  Paul was in prison in Rome during Emperor Nero's reign and died in AD 68. This was a savage, brutal time, and Nero was a terrible leader. Paul was a Roman citizen, and according to tradition, he was taken from prison and beheaded on the third mile marker of the Ostian Way.

- Who were the four people that Paul particularly missed?

  Paul mentioned his fellow worker Demas, who had deserted him for Thessalonica because he had apparently fallen away spiritually. Paul also said that Crescens had gone to Galatia, Titus had traveled to Dalmatia, and Tychicus had been sent to Ephesus. We don't have a lot of details about all these men, but it does seem that many of them were busy serving the Lord for the sake of the gospel.

Paul's Practical and Spiritual Longings

- In the 1500s, who wrote a letter with a request like Paul's, and why?

  William Tyndale wrote a letter from his prison cell in 1535. Unlike Paul's letter to a friend and protégé, Tyndale's letter was written to the governor of Vilvoorde, where Tyndale was imprisoned. He asked the governor if he would be so kind as to allow him to have his goods, including a warmer cap, a warmer coat, and cloth to repair his leggings, since it appeared that he was to spend the winter in the cold prison cell. At the end, he also made a plea for his Bible and lexicon, that he might continue to study.

- What was significant about Paul's wanting "the parchments" (2 Tim. 4:13)?

  Even though Paul was facing death, it wasn't a time for him to stop learning, studying, and growing. He wanted to read and grow in his understanding. Dr. Thomas concludes that Paul may have even been trying to prepare another letter that was on his heart. Regardless of the precise motives, it is clear that Paul was a man who loved the Word of God.

- When everyone else deserted Paul at his trial, who stood by him?

  Paul said that at his first trial, no one had come to his defense. We know that Luke was present; Dr. Thomas speculates that Luke may have been unable to help because he was a doctor rather than a lawyer. The Lord was the One who "stood by [Paul] and strengthened [him]" (2 Tim. 4:17). Paul knew the presence of God and the power of the Holy Spirit as he faced trial. Paul had the ultimate defense—the Lord Jesus Christ.

After the Video

- What did the Apostle Paul do, knowing that his death was imminent? What does this teach us?

  Even though Paul knew that the end of his life was near, he didn't give up. He didn't throw a pity party or try to enjoy the last moments he had (however one might try to enjoy them in a prison cell). Paul was faithful until the end. Paul used his last days to build up the faith of Timothy and continue laying the foundation of discipleship that he had begun. Paul was still focused on his mission: proclaiming the gospel of Jesus Christ. Paul's attitude toward the last days of his life should be sobering for all of us as believers. We should not live on mission and then see our final days as rest. We should pursue Christ and the proclamation of the gospel until our dying breath, just like the Apostle Paul.

- What was so meaningful about Paul's request that Timothy come to him along with John Mark, and what is the lesson in this for us?

  Paul's request that Timothy bring John Mark along should not be overlooked. It is no insignificant detail because Paul and John Mark had had a falling-out and had parted ways because Paul no longer wanted to do missionary work together. The fact that Paul asked for John Mark to come and visit him indicates that they had restored their relationship. For us, this is a lesson in the importance of mending relationships, especially before death. But since we do not know the day or hour of our death or that of anyone else, we ought to always strive to keep short accounts. Walking in reconciled and restored relationships is a beautiful gift of God's grace to the believer whenever it is possible.

- What can we learn from both Paul's asking Timothy to bring him his cloak and Timothy's willingness to answer this request?

  In this instance, both Paul and Timothy demonstrated humility. Paul was an Apostle, but in this moment, he humbled himself to acknowledge his basic needs. He was human, a mere man; he needed his cloak for warmth. He didn't try to tough out the winter and act as though he were impervious to harsh conditions. He humbly admitted his need. Timothy also demonstrated humility because he was not above the task. Paul asked him because he knew that his request would be met with a humble servant's heart. Often, we can struggle with either side of this exchange. In our pride, we can resist admitting our humanity and our need. It requires humility to ask for help, especially in the so-called small things that we think we can handle on our own. On the other hand, we can also respond in pride when asked to serve in simple, practical, mundane kinds of ways. We need to humbly accept opportunities to serve in these ways, focusing more on the giving than on the glory we get from serving in big, visible ways.

REVIEW QUIZ

1. **B.**
   Paul was imprisoned three times that we are aware of, but there may have been other occasions that Luke did not record in the book of Acts. We know that Paul was imprisoned in Philippi early in his ministry. In AD 62, Paul was imprisoned in Rome during what was more of a house arrest, and then Paul was imprisoned again in Rome in around 67.

2. **D.**
   Onesiphorus was a faithful brother and servant of the Lord. Paul described him as one who "often refreshed [him]" (2 Tim. 1:16). It seems that Onesiphorus made it his aim to encourage and refresh Paul based on the fact that "when he arrived in Rome

he searched for [Paul] earnestly" (v. 17). Onesiphorus was not ashamed or afraid of the potential cost to serve the Apostle.

3. **A.**
   Timothy was Paul's protégé in the faith. It was Timothy to whom Paul was writing a second letter during this time of imprisonment. The fact that Paul was writing to Timothy at this time indicates what a special relationship they had. Paul got personal with Timothy, and in addition to several greetings, Paul made several requests and shared what he would like in his final days.

4. **A.**
   While Paul had several visitors throughout his imprisonment, it was Luke who was present with him. Luke was most likely not in the prison with Paul, but Luke was able to attend to Paul's needs, visit him, and minister to him. Eubulus, Pudens, and Linus were mentioned by Paul as visitors he'd previously had and been encouraged by.

5. **C.**
   The parchments probably included Hebrew texts of the Old Testament, and although Paul would have likely had large portions of it memorized, he still wanted to read the texts. Perhaps he wanted to read and consult passages less familiar to him to study and prepare for another letter on his mind.

6. **B.**
   Paul never stated that he missed his freedom. At other times, he said that his imprisonment was useful for the advancement of the gospel and that he trusted the Lord's providence. He did miss his companions, his clothes, the parchments, and God's presence.

11

God's Vision to John on Patmos

INTRODUCTION

Imagine being banished to a remote island on account of your faith, having to find food and shelter with no hope of escape. Imagine that you are in your eighties when this happens. This is where we find the Apostle John in the book of Revelation. We find not a man full of complaint in his hardships but a man full of worship of his glorious Savior. In this lesson, Dr. Thomas describes the conditions of John's imprisonment, his focus in his last days, and his experience with the Spirit of God and the Lord Jesus Christ.

LEARNING GOALS

When you have finished this lesson, you should be able to:

- Describe John's imprisonment on the island of Patmos
- Understand the significance of John's focus and experience
- Better understand the glory and holiness of Jesus Christ in order to worship Him more fully

KEY IDEAS

- Sabbath rest and worship are rhythms established by God.
- Believers are indwelt by the Holy Spirit and should be in tune with the Spirit.
- Worship of the living, true God is first vertical, where there is something to be felt and experienced in the presence of God.
- John was given a profound vision of Christ, and we get a glimpse into the majesty and holiness of Christ through John's writing.

REFLECTION & DISCUSSION QUESTIONS

Before the Video

What Do You Think?

Take a moment to answer the following questions. They will prepare you for the lecture.

- How do you cope with hardship?

- How would you describe worship as an experience?

Scripture Reading

Blessed is the one who reads aloud the words of this prophecy, and blessed are those who hear, and who keep what is written in it, for the time is near.

—Revelation 1:3

- Revelation is a book that many people shy away from because of the difficulty in understanding it, but according to this verse, what is promised to the one who reads it? Why do you think the reader is promised this?

During the Video

Answer the following questions while you watch the video. They will guide you through the lecture.

John's Setting *0:00–10:41*

- Where was the island of Patmos, and what was it like?

- How did the rhythm of work and rest change from the old covenant to the new covenant?

John's Experience *10:41–22:57*

- What did John mean when he said that he was "in the Spirit" in Revelation 1:10?

- Since John was an Apostle, what unique aspects of being in the Spirit did he have?

- What did John see, and how did he respond?

- What did John hear?

After the Video

Answer the following questions after you have finished the lecture. They will help you identify and summarize the major points.

- What is the Christian Sabbath?

  If you are in a group, have the members discuss the importance of Sabbath rhythms and how they might think differently about rest and incorporate these patterns into their lives.

- We live in a culture that values experience. How does the true Christian worship experience differ from what Dr. Thomas describes as a church culture of "seeker sensitivity"?

  If you are in a group, have the members discuss ways that they have resisted falling into an experiential-worship mentality on the Lord's Day.

- What things occupied John in his imprisonment?

  If you are in a group, have the members discuss what things tend to occupy them and how they might realign their hearts to be occupied with what the Apostle John was enraptured with.

PRAYER

Commit what you have learned from God's Word in this lesson to prayer.

- Praise God that through John's vision, we get a glimpse into Christ as our Prophet, Priest, and King.
- Confess ways in which you have not been worshiping God in spirit and in truth.
- Thank God for the blessings that come through reading His Word, specifically the book of Revelation.
- Ask God to help you grow in being more conscious of the Lord's Day.

REVIEW QUIZ

Use these multiple-choice questions to measure what you learned from this lesson.

1. When was the book of Revelation written, according to Dr. Thomas?
   a. The book was written in the late 30s.
   b. The book was written in the early 90s.
   c. The book was written in the mid- to late 60s.
   d. The book was written in the late 120s.

2. Who were the "Sons of Thunder"?
   a. James and John
   b. Herod Agrippa and Herod Antipas
   c. Emperor Nero and Emperor Domitian
   d. John the son of Boanerges and John the Baptist

3. As John began the book of Revelation, what was he aware of?
   a. That it was the Lord's Day
   b. That his release was imminent
   c. That he was being executed the following day
   d. That the churches were asking for him to write

4. What was Jesus' favorite self-designation?
   a. Savior
   b. Christ
   c. Son of Man
   d. Son of God

5. John's description of Jesus highlighted the threefold office of Christ, known as the *munus triplex*.
   a. True
   b. False

6. Who said, "There is not a square inch of the whole dominion of our human existence over which Christ, who is sovereign of all, does not cry: 'Mine!' "?
   a. Abraham Kuyper
   b. John Calvin
   c. Martin Luther
   d. R.C. Sproul

Answer Key—God's Vision to John on Patmos

REFLECTION & DISCUSSION QUESTIONS

Before the Video

What Do You Think?

These are personal questions. The answers should be based on your own knowledge and experience.

Scripture Reading

- Revelation is a book that many people shy away from because of the difficulty in understanding it, but according to this verse, what is promised to the one who reads it? Why do you think the reader is promised this?

  While this lesson is not an exhaustive study on Revelation, it's worth noting that the Apostle John begins by stating that there is blessing for the one who reads, hears, and keeps these words. It's logical to conclude, then, that if we are not reading Revelation, we are missing out. Even in this opening chapter, we can see some of the blessing. John shares his vision of Christ. Through reading this, we gain a better understanding of Christ's power and holiness. We are drawn into greater understanding of truth and a greater emotional response in our spirits, causing us to worship the Lamb in spirit and in truth. That is just one blessing of reading the first few verses of the book of Revelation.

During the Video

John's Setting

- Where was the island of Patmos, and what was it like?

  The island of Patmos is one of the Aegean islands located southwest of modern-day Turkey. It's thirteen square miles of rock and caves, barren of any vegetation. There would have been very few buildings at the time of John's imprisonment; what buildings there were would have been used by the Roman soldiers. Prisoners would have lived in the caves and would probably have caught their own fish for food. It was a desolate place, perfect for keeping prisoners.

- How did the rhythm of work and rest change from the old covenant to the new covenant?

  The old covenant began with work and ended with rest. The first six days of the week were devoted to work, and the final day of the week was the Sabbath, a day of rest. But in the new covenant, rest is followed by work. Dr. Thomas notes that this may be a gospel pattern that ushered in the change. The Lord's Day was observed on Sunday as a celebration of the resurrection of Jesus Christ.

John's Experience

- What did John mean when he said that he was "in the Spirit" in Revelation 1:10?

  The Holy Spirit is the third person of the Trinity, the representative agent of Christ. Jesus promised to send the Spirit after He had ascended to the Father. When John made this statement, he was saying that he was indwelled by the Spirit. This carries all the benefits of being in the Spirit, which includes being taught, nourished, filled, and even being rebuked by the Spirit. John was listening to the Spirit of God and was in tune with Him.

- Since John was an Apostle, what unique aspects of being in the Spirit did he have?

  In addition to the benefits of the indwelling of the Holy Spirit that all believers receive, John had some unique aspects that we don't possess. He had visions and inspiration. He was directly told by Jesus in Revelation to write down what he witnessed, which was the process of inscripturation.

- What did John see, and how did he respond?

  John saw Jesus, the Son of Man, in a vision. John used apocalyptic language to describe what he saw. Jesus was dressed in a robe with a golden sash around His chest. He had white, snowy hair and a blazing fire coming out of His eyes. His feet were glowing like bronze in a furnace. This was a profound image that John saw, and his response was like that of the prophet Isaiah. Overwhelmed by the sight of Jesus' glory and holiness, John fell at Jesus' feet.

- What did John hear?

  Jesus spoke these words of comfort, hope, and promise to John: "Fear not, I am the first and the last, and the living one. I died, and behold I am alive forevermore, and I have the keys of Death and Hades" (Rev. 1:17–18). As John was facing imminent death, Jesus reminded John that He is the One who holds the keys to life and death, He is the One who died to forgive sins, and He is the One we can trust. There was nothing for John to fear.

After the Video

- What is the Christian Sabbath?

  Sabbath is part of the new covenant as well as of the old. While the ceremonial aspects of Sabbath were done away with in the new covenant, Dr. Thomas argues that the keeping of a special day of the week remains the same. This commandment was not done away with while the other nine remain. Though some have suggested that the Sabbath rest is fulfilled because of the rest we now have in

Christ, Jeremiah 31, which is quoted in Hebrews, states that the law is written on the hearts and minds of believers. This includes the fourth commandment. A special day of the week ought to be set aside—Sunday, in remembrance of Christ's resurrection—to be with the people of God and worship Him at the outset of the week.

- We live in a culture that values experience. How does the true Christian worship experience differ from what Dr. Thomas describes as a church culture of "seeker sensitivity"?

  The mindset of the modern church is consumeristic. The biggest question on people's minds is: "What's in it for me?" If it doesn't meet "my" needs or make "me" feel happy, then it's not worthwhile. This is a sad and unfortunate reality because it's the opposite of how we are to approach the living, triune God. Worship is not about us; it's about God. Worship is vertical. This does not mean that worship is a stuffy, emotionless, experience-less activity. Dr. Thomas points out that John had a worship experience. His senses were engaged, and his heart was engaged. When Jesus addressed the Samaritan woman, He approached her on the question of worship, challenging her that we are all created to worship the true, living God in spirit and truth. We often err on one side or the other, but God wants spirit and *truth in our worship.*

- What things occupied John in his imprisonment?

  While John was in exile in his eighties and facing his death, he was still consumed with Jesus. John was concerned with worship and the Lord's Day. Like Paul, who was faithful to the end, John was still a man on mission. He had been given a job to do, and he was going to faithfully do it. He wrote down the things that he saw and heard, writing to the churches in Asia Minor. He did not give up in his final days on the island of Patmos because his heart was set on worshiping Jesus, driving him to press on even in tribulation and trials.

REVIEW QUIZ

1. **B.**
   The date of Revelation is debated. Dr. Sproul held the view that it was written in the mid- to late 60s before Titus destroyed the city of Jerusalem, thus placing the events prophesied in much of Revelation in the near future, these events being written about during the reign of Nero (54–68). Dr. Thomas holds to a later date, that many of these events would be fulfilled under Emperor Domitian's reign, placing the date of John's writing Revelation in the early 90s.

2. **A.**
   John, the son of Boanerges, had a brother named James. These two were known as the "Sons of Thunder." Both these men suffered persecution. James was arrested and killed by Herod Agrippa, while John was later arrested in Ephesus and banished to the island of Patmos, living to an old age.

3. **A.**
   In Revelation 1:10, John says that he was "in the Spirit on the Lord's day." John was fully conscious of the fact that it was the Lord's Day. Dr. Thomas points out how remarkable this was because John would have had no calendar or form of technology to know this, which makes us understand the great importance of the Lord's Day for early Christians.

4. **C.**
   Jesus' favorite self-designation was "Son of Man." Dr. Thomas notes that when Jesus said, "For even the Son of Man came not to be served but to serve, and to give His life as a ransom for many" (Mark 10:45).

5. **A.**
   The threefold office of Christ is that of Prophet, Priest, and King. John's description of Jesus highlighted each of these aspects of the Messiah. From Christ's responsibilities to His garments, He is depicted as the Prophet, Priest, and King. As Dr. Thomas states, the image of Christ here is profound. These aspects of Christ's office are full of rich, deep truths for the believer to ponder.

6. **A.**
   Kuyper stated that Christ proclaims "Mine" over everything in creation and every aspect of our existence. Jesus Christ is the One who is ruling and reigning. He is in control, and He is in control of all. He is worthy of our entire lives.

12

God's Power in Jesus Christ

INTRODUCTION

The last imprisonment in this series may be a little surprising, since it is not what you might think of as an imprisonment. In this final lesson, Dr. Thomas takes an in-depth look at the arrest, trial, crucifixion, and burial of the Lord Jesus Christ. While we might not think of these events as an imprisonment, there are profound truths to be learned in these moments about apostasy, the fulfillment of Scripture, and the gospel.

LEARNING GOALS

When you have finished this lesson, you should be able to:

- Explain the events of Jesus' arrest, trial, crucifixion, and burial
- Describe the process of apostasy
- Understand why you ought to preach the gospel to yourself regularly
- Develop a deeper understanding of your sinfulness and the wonder of the atonement

KEY IDEAS

- Jesus' betrayal, arrest, crucifixion, and burial were all in fulfillment of Scripture.
- If Judas, who spent years in close proximity to Christ, could harden his heart and reject Christ, we must all take heed lest we fall.
- Jesus bore the full weight of God's wrath for our sin.
- Jesus conquered sin and death by rising victoriously from the grave.

REFLECTION & DISCUSSION QUESTIONS

Before the Video

What Do You Think?

Take a moment to answer the following questions. They will prepare you for the lecture.

- Describe the events leading up to Jesus' betrayal and arrest.

- How do you think Jesus was imprisoned?

Scripture Reading

For our sake he made him to be sin who knew no sin, so that in him we might become the righteousness of God.

—2 Corinthians 5:21

- What does it mean that God made Christ "to be sin" for us, and what are the implications of this?

During the Video

Answer the following questions while you watch the video. They will guide you through the lecture.

The Betrayal and Arrest of Christ *0:00–9:38*

- Why is it significant that Jesus was betrayed in a garden?

- What is the significance of Mark's noting Jesus' statement "But let the Scriptures be fulfilled" (14:49)?

- How did Judas get to the point of betraying Jesus?

The Trial, Crucifixion, and Burial of Christ *9:38–23:39*

- In what ways can we call Jesus' trial unjust?

- How did Jesus respond during His trial, and why did He respond this way?

- It was common for crucifixions to last for several days, but Jesus died quickly. What might have been part of the reason for this?

After the Video

Answer the following questions after you have finished the lecture. They will help you identify and summarize the major points.

- What is the importance of preaching the gospel to yourself every day?

  If you are in a group, have the members discuss some practical ways that they currently do this or can start doing it.

- What is the significance of J.S. Bach's retelling of Jesus' trial in his *St. Matthew Passion*? How does understanding this reality shape our perspective of God and ourselves?

  If you are in a group, have the members discuss the reasons that they don't want to see this reality or why it's hard to acknowledge it to others.

- As we conclude this series, consider the people we've studied, their experiences of imprisonment, and the lessons they learned. What are some of the themes you've seen throughout the lessons?

  If you are in a group, have the members review the characters together and the greatest lessons that they have learned through this series.

PRAYER

Commit what you have learned from God's Word in this lesson to prayer.

- Praise God for the atoning sacrifice of Christ and His righteousness with which we are clothed if we trust Him.
- Confess any ways that you have taken the crucifixion of Christ lightly.
- Thank God that there is no wrath for you in Christ—only mercy and grace.
- Ask God to grant you a deeper understanding of and appreciation for the gospel.

REVIEW QUIZ

Use these multiple-choice questions to measure what you learned from this lesson.

1. Who were the Zealots?
   a. Comrades of Judas who helped plot Christ's arrest
   b. Avid followers of the Pharisees and the Sanhedrin
   c. Disciples who were zealous to follow Jesus no matter the cost
   d. Insurrectionists who wanted to overthrow Roman power

2. Judas bowed before Jesus so that the temple police could identify Him.
   a. True
   b. False

3. According to the warnings of apostasy in Hebrews 3, what can cause the hardening of a person's heart?
   a. The deceitfulness of sin
   b. The deceitfulness of false teachers
   c. The deceitfulness of other apostates
   d. The deceitfulness of incorrect theology

4. According to C.S. Lewis, what changed from ancient to modern times regarding man's approach to God?
   a. God used to be esteemed as transcendent, but now He is treated without regard for His holiness.
   b. God used to be Judge, but now man has positioned himself as judge.
   c. God used to be feared, but now people fear others more.
   d. God used to be worshiped, but now He is cursed.

5. During the trial and the time leading up to His crucifixion, Jesus was greatly mistreated. Which of the following was *not* one of the ways that Jesus was mistreated?
   a. He had a crown of thorns placed on His head.
   b. He was offered sour wine to drink.
   c. He was hit and spat on.
   d. He was mocked.

6. According to Dr. Thomas, what was Jesus' form of incarceration?
   a. Having an unjust trial
   b. Taking on human flesh
   c. Being buried in a tomb
   d. Being crucified on a cross

Answer Key—God's Power in Jesus Christ

REFLECTION & DISCUSSION QUESTIONS

Before the Video

What Do You Think?

These are personal questions. The answers should be based on your own knowledge and experience.

Scripture Reading

- What does it mean that God made Christ "to be sin" for us, and what are the implications of this?

  Christ took our sins upon Himself on the cross and bore the full weight of the wrath of God for those sins. According to Martin Luther's description, Christ was the greatest sinner in that moment. That was not because of His own sin; Christ was sinless—the spotless Lamb of God. But on the cross, God the Father treated Him as though He were a sinner, so that He could bear our sin and we could receive His righteousness instead of the wrath of God that we deserved. It was the great exchange—our sin for His righteousness.

During the Video

The Betrayal and Arrest of Christ

- Why is it significant that Jesus was betrayed in a garden?

  The opening pages of Scripture began in a garden—it was perfect, beautiful, and untainted. Sin was ushered into the world by Adam and Eve in the garden of Eden. There is another garden at the end of Scripture, however, when Jesus Christ, the second Adam, will restore everything and make it new. It is only fitting that the betrayal of Jesus took place in a garden because the two gardens bookend the whole of redemptive history.

- What is the significance of Mark's noting Jesus' statement "But let the Scriptures be fulfilled" (14:49)?

  Jesus commented that there had been plenty of opportunities for His arrest before that moment in the garden of Gethsemane. Jesus had taught in the temple many times, yet they hadn't seized Him. Jesus went on to say that the Scriptures needed to be fulfilled—the completion of Jesus' ministry, suffering, and obedience to the Father had to take place. Everything happened up to this point, during this point, and after this point in accordance with Scripture and the will of the Father.

- How did Judas get to the point of betraying Jesus?

  Dr. Thomas describes apostasy as a change that occurred in Judas' heart. Judas' apostasy didn't happen overnight. Judas was one of the twelve disciples. He had followed Jesus, and months and years before his betrayal, he never would have agreed with statements that he would betray Jesus. The other disciples never suspected him either. But something happened. Something happened that caused him to sear his conscience and become desensitized. Judas' heart was hardened and calloused to the point that he walked away from the faith, even though he was in close proximity with Jesus as a disciple.

The Trial, Crucifixion, and Burial of Christ

- In what ways can we call Jesus' trial unjust?

  At this time, Rome permitted the Jews to have some control over judiciary matters in the temple and even over civilian issues. This case with Jesus was a capital one, and the meeting should not have been at night. The meeting should have taken place at the temple, not at the high priest's house. Witnesses were to be given opportunity to be warned against rumors, and there were to be multiple witnesses in agreement. In this case, the witnesses did not agree in their testimony. False evidence and false testimonies were brought forward without proper examination.

- How did Jesus respond during His trial, and why did He respond this way?

  Jesus remained silent at first (Mark 14:61) and then answered in agreement that He was the Christ (v. 62). Christ did not defend Himself against all the false accusations or the injustices. He humbly submitted and gave Himself in full obedience as the ransom for many. He allowed the fulfillment of prophecy regarding His trial and execution to unfold. This was part of His victory fight against darkness, against sin, against His crucifixion, and against the tomb.

- It was common for crucifixions to last for several days, but Jesus died quickly. What might have been part of the reason for this?

  When Jesus was crucified, He died by that evening. This was not typical, and Dr. Thomas connects it to Jesus' being under the wrath of God. There is no way to know the full extent of what Christ bore physically because of the crushing burden of the wrath of God. We know that Christ felt intense agony. He felt a physical and spiritual removal of God's presence. Jesus cried out to God, not even calling Him "My Father," as He hung on a cross as a condemned sinner.

After the Video

- What is the importance of preaching the gospel to yourself every day?

  Dr. Thomas exhorts believers to preach the gospel to themselves every day. We need to remind ourselves daily that it is only by trusting in Jesus and Jesus alone that we have any hope of salvation. Preaching the gospel to ourselves each day has other benefits as well. It anchors our identity and hope to Christ. The reality of who we are as Christ's as laid out in Ephesians 1 realigns our hearts and perspectives so that we might live each day from a gospel-motivated and grace-driven position.

- What is the significance of J.S. Bach's retelling of Jesus' trial in his *St. Matthew Passion*? How does understanding this reality shape our perspective of God and ourselves?

  In Matthew's account of Jesus' trial, the onlookers mocked Jesus by blindfolding Him, hitting Him, and asking Him who had done it. In Bach's retelling of this in the St. Matthew Passion, *the choir responds to the question "Who is it that hit you?" with "I, I and my sins." By including the response of "I, I and my sins," Bach was in essence rightly proclaiming the gospel. Jesus Christ went to the cross to save sinners. It wasn't just those false accusers on the night of Jesus' trial who sent Him to His execution on the cross. It was you; it was me. If we remove ourselves from the events of the gospel story, we remove ourselves and our sin as reasons that Christ had to die. This is a sobering and humbling reality, but when we rightly understand our sinfulness, we rightly understand our need for a Savior and will grasp the undeserved mercy and love that He bestows on us with humility and gratitude.*

- As we conclude this series, consider the people we've studied, their experiences of imprisonment, and the lessons they learned. What are some of the themes you've seen throughout the lessons?

  Answers may vary based on individual reflections. One of the themes throughout the lessons is God's sovereignty. While this was especially considered in the life of Joseph and the evil done to him that God used for good, there are traces of God's sovereignty throughout all these stories. We saw God's providential hand working behind the scenes, using unexpected people and unexpected circumstances to bring about His purposes, His glory, and the good of His people. Consider Job's declaration in Job 42:2: "I know that you can do all things, and that no purpose of yours can be thwarted." This is our God. He is a God who providentially weaves all the details of our lives. He uses imprisonments of various kinds for various reasons and for varying lengths for the furtherance of the gospel so that we might be people refined and more transformed into His image.

REVIEW QUIZ

1. **D.**
   The Zealots were a group of insurrectionists who wanted to rise up and take power back from Rome through military force. One of Jesus' disciples was Simon the Zealot. This may have created some fear that the disciples were insurrectionists, but there's no indication that Simon still followed that path once he became a disciple of Jesus.

2. **B.**
   There could be various reasons why the temple police needed a sign. It could have had to do with the darkness. Whatever the exact reason, we know they needed a sign. Judas chose a sign that truly displayed betrayal. He chose to kiss Jesus, identifying Him to the soldiers as the One to arrest in the darkness of the garden.

3. **A.**
   Hebrews 3:13 says, "But exhort one another every day, as long as it is called 'today,' that none of you may be hardened by the deceitfulness of sin." This is a very sober warning. Believers should never underestimate the power of sin. Part of the reason for sin's power is its deception. May God grant us soft hearts with tender consciences, that we might not be deceived by sin.

4. **B.**
   In ancient times, man approached God like an accused person approaching a judge. In modern times, however, the roles have reversed—man treats God like the accused One and himself as the judge. People now question God, asking Him to provide a reasonable defense for Himself.

5. **B.**
   Leading up to His crucifixion, Jesus experienced severe mockery. He was clothed with purple robes and had a crown of thorns placed on His head while being called "King of the Jews." He was also hit and spat upon. He was even stripped of His clothing. This was all just leading up to His agonizing crucifixion. It was on the cross that He was offered sour wine.

6. **C.**
   Dr. Thomas describes the burial of the Lord Jesus Christ as the greatest incarceration. Jesus—the Lord of life—experienced death and was buried in a tomb. Death and burial are not natural; they were never to have been and are only the result of sin. Praise God, Jesus did not remain in the grave. He burst forth from that prison of a tomb and rose victoriously over death.